some day You will No all about me.

so me day you will No all about me.

YOUNG CHILDREN'S EXPLORATIONS IN THE WORLD OF LETTERS

ANNE ROBINSON

Manchester
Polytechnic,
England

LESLIE CRAWFORD

Moorhead
State University,
Minnesota, USA

NIGEL HALL

Manchester
Polytechnic,
England

N igel

Mrs. Robinson

Les

Heinemann
Portsmouth New Hampshire

Heinemann Educational Books, Inc.
361 Hanover Street, Portsmouth, NH 03801-3959
Offices and agents throughout the world

Library of Congress Cataloging-in-Publication Data
Robinson, Anne.
Some day you will no (sic) all about me: young
children's explorations in the world of letters/ Anne
Robinson. Leslie Crawford, Nigel Hall.
p. cm.
Includes bibliographical references (p. 127)
ISBN 0-435-08549-2: $15.00
1. Pen pals – United States.   2. Pen pals – Great Britain.
3. Letter-writing.   I. Crawford, Leslie.   II. Hall, Nigel.
III. Title.   IV. Some day you will no all about me.
LB3614.R63   1991
372.6 23—dc20
90-49192
CIP

First published in North America 1991 by Heinemann
Educational Books, Inc. First published in 1990 by
Mary Glasgow Publications Ltd., Avenue House,
131-133 Holland Park Avenue, London W11 4UT,
England.

ISBN 0-435-08549-2

Printed in Great Britain
by St Edmundsbury Press Limited,
Bury St Edmunds, Suffolk

CONTENTS

ACKNOWLEDGEMENTS

This book would not have been possible without considerable support from many people. We would like to thank Rob Greenall and Finian O'Shea for reading some of the manuscript, and Nick Hutchins for having faith in it. We would like to thank the parents of all the children for their continued support. We are very grateful to Margaret Shearing and Martin Popplewell, the class teachers who so enthusiastically continued with and supported the exchange. The letters would have foundered many times if it had not been for the patience, care and concern of the headteacher, Bernice Magson, who so willingly allowed us into her school. Finally, but most important, our debt to the children is enormous. They have taken part in the exchange wholeheartedly and have put up with all our delays, intrusions and questions. Throughout this book, their voices can be heard over and over again. These voices are fresh, dynamic and fascinating. We only hope that we have been able to do justice to the effort, the power, and the humanity of the children's authorship.

INTRODUCTION

This is a book about letter writing in action. It is not a book about how to teach letter writing; there are no prescriptions, no rules and no instructions. It is the story of a group of 20 children, each of whom corresponded with an adult from the age of 5½ years. It is the story of how the exchanges began and how they developed. It is the story of how these children changed as authors of letters, how they coped with writing to a distant, relatively unknown audience, and how they developed a relationship with their correspondent almost solely through the words that they wrote and read.

We cannot claim that all children would respond as these children did. What we do claim is that, given an authentic authoring experience, these children became enthusiastic correspondents who have sustained their commitment fully during, and beyond, the two-year period covered by this book.

We have as far as possible told our story without the formality of conventional academic writing. We have left any theoretical comments until the final chapter. We felt that reading and thinking about the correspondence should have priority over setting it in a wider educational perspective.

While this book is not about teaching letter writing, it contains an important message for those working with young authors. It is that authentic, purposeful and sustained opportunities to function as authors provide the most satisfying, most rewarding, most valued, and ultimately the most beneficial learning experiences. Such experiences are not optional extras. They are the very essence of successful learning.

CHAPTER ONE

and I ll allways be your freind

THE HISTORY OF THE LETTER EXCHANGE

This story started when the three authors met at a time that each of them was interested in exploring ways of developing children's interest in writing. Anne Robinson was a college lecturer who had returned to the classroom for one year. Nigel Hall was also a college lecturer, and Leslie Crawford was a visiting American professor working with him.

Towards the end of 1986 our interests in young children's authorship were beginning to converge. We did not perceive authorship as the consequence of mechanical and routinised skill-based activities. Our reading, our research, and our extensive involvement with young children had convinced us that children, from the start, bring to the authoring process their experience, ability and a commitment to imparting meaning. It was not appropriate to think of authorship as something which happened after children had learned to write neatly and to spell correctly. We knew that young children were able to function as authors from the beginning and that it was experience of authorship which led to the refinement of writing. Central to our concern were certain principles:

- That children have the ultimate responsibility for what they write. They are the authorities on their writing. It is no accident that 'author' and 'authority' are related terms.

- That authorship is given a certain bite if the writer understands that an audience exists, and if that audience is interested in, and cares about, the meanings generated by the writer.

- That the most convincing demonstration of an interest in, and care for, a child's writing is to respond to it by using the same medium. In other words, for the reader to give a concrete commitment to a response.

- That some writing tasks for children are intrinsically difficult because they involve genres whose demands will not be familiar. Dialogue journals and letters are less difficult because, although unfamiliar to many children, they allow children to write with their own voices. Writers are not made to look inadequate by a failure to understand literary genre conventions.

Anne had been putting the first three principles into operation in her classroom. The children she taught had little experience of reading schemes. They always read from good children's books and shared them with friends, teachers and parents. They did not do any systematic phonic work and had never encountered the sterile exercises of workbooks. The children's writing was never graded but was always responded to and commented on, often with further written comments. The children did not use erasers and were not instructed in spelling, although frequent discussion occurred while their work was in progress. Anne's role was always to support, discuss, help evaluate, question, and encourage.

In order to increase our understanding of young children's authorship, we decided to see whether the children in Anne's class would be willing to correspond with Les and Nigel.

To clarify what kind of exchange of letters this was going to be, we identified what were for us three important conditions:

1   *Written dialogue is only significant if it extends over time.*

We were not interested in one-off letters. Such letters are important but we felt that real exploration with written language between correspondents has to develop over time. Participants need to have the chance to get to know each other, to develop a style of exchange, and to understand the obligations of sustained communication.

2   *In written dialogue, each participant must have equal rights.*

Although Les and Nigel, as mature writers, clearly had competencies much greater than the children, they were not entitled to use that competence in a didactic way. It was not their function to control the dialogue. They were partners in an exchange.

3   *In written dialogue, it is the meanings which are significant rather than the form.*

Friends do not normally correct, mark, or grade each other's letters. They write because they have important or interesting things to say to each other; they want to know about each other's lives. Each accepts the other's letters as they are. Friends do not seek to embarrass or humiliate each other.

Anne began to think about how the exchange would be introduced to the children. Because this activity would extend beyond school and involve people who were not known to the children or staff, she had to seek formal permission. It was decided that the parents should be informed and they were sent this letter explaining what was going to happen:

Dear Parents

As part of my work to help the children become more fluent writers, I am getting two of my colleagues from Manchester Polytechnic to start letter writing with the children. The children will write to them at the Polytechnic and my colleagues will write back. In this way we hope to encourage the children to develop their communication skills. My colleagues are Nigel Hall from the Department of Education Studies, and Professor Leslie Crawford, Visiting Fellow to the School of Education. I would be interested to hear from any of you about the children's reactions to their letter writing experiences.

The parents were already involved in their children's literacy development through general interest and support at home. The children took books home each evening to share with their parents. Because of this, and other involvements with the parents, we did not anticipate any problems.

Preparations also had to be made in the classroom. Anne decided to start with a topic on 'Communication'. She had been waiting for an appropriate time to introduce a new book, *The Jolly Postman*, by J and A Ahlberg and thought it could also be used to introduce the children to letter writing. The children, like all children, loved *The Jolly Postman* and needed only a suggestion from Anne to have a go at writing letters to some of the characters.

We then decided that Les and Nigel would visit the classroom, meet the children, and give each child an initial letter. We must admit that a major part of the strategy was for Les and Nigel to make a substantial impact upon the consciousness of the children. This visit would be the only face-to-face contact for some time, and we were quite concerned that the children should have a pleasant and interesting image of the two adults to carry in their minds.

We worked carefully on the content and wording of the first letter, which would be addressed to each child and signed individually by either Les or Nigel (see chapter 2). All that remained was for Les and Nigel to make their visit and distribute the letters.

Anne thought it would be best if the children followed their normal classroom routine: one group working in the math area, one in the craft area, a third in the socio-dramatic play area, and the fourth in the writing area. Nothing new or ambitious was planned in the way of class activities as Anne anticipated being involved to some extent with Nigel and Les when they were in the classroom.

From Anne's perspective as the teacher, she reported that two things stood out about the visit:

One was the excitement of the whole class. It was a special event and somehow different from when other adult visitors came into the room. This was partly due to Les and Nigel not behaving like the 'normal' visitors we had. Les and Nigel managed to cause chaos by sitting on the rug with the children and insisting on having their names called out when I did the register. The second, but perhaps related, aspect was the quality of the relationship which developed between the children and their visitors. They joined children at work and at play, and I was not always certain what was going on, but by the end of the morning my class knew that they had found two new friends.

Nigel and Les were also buoyed up by the success of the visit. Both of them were relieved that the children had responded well to them. That the visit had been a success was confirmed a year later when Anne talked to some of the children about their memories of the visit. The children still had a vivid recollection of what had happened:

We just saw two men sitting on the carpet.

Yes, Les was sitting on the carpet and everyone was hugging him.

I was surprised because we had not seen them before and they had written letters to us all.

Nigel brought a movie camera.

The crucial question was whether the enthusiasm would continue. Would the children actually write any letters? We had agreed that there was to be no compulsion to take part; no-one had to reply if they did not want to. Anne was prepared to remind the children if necessary but no pressure was to be put upon them to respond. As it turned out, reminders were not needed.

Anne wrote down what happened:

During the next week the children came to take their turn in the writing area. The letters from Nigel and Les were looked at again, the visit remembered and the children wrote back. I explained that they could decide what they wanted to say in their letters and that, when they had finished, they should bring them to me and I would collect them all together for posting onwards. I realised that some of the letters had parts that would be difficult for Les and Nigel to read, so each child was invited to read their letters to me. Later, before posting, I added some translations or information which would allow more sense to be made of them. Every single one of the

children wanted to write and none of them asked for ideas or information.

The completed letters were bundled up and posted on to Les and Nigel. The three of us had decided that there should be very few concessions to the children's age or experience. Les and Nigel would try to write neatly but, as far as possible, would use the kinds of expressions and language that they would with other adult correspondents. We decided that the letters should be kept relatively short in the first instance but that the length would subsequently be a function of each individual exchange. Les and Nigel were to be free to write about all aspects of their lives but we agreed that it was legitimate to write more about what the children could easily understand.

Les found some initial difficulties in dealing with his letters:

I felt I had some unique problems in responding to the letters. My background was different. In particular, I had different expressions, spellings, and handwriting which might limit children's understanding. I decided to adapt my language, spelling and handwriting to better conform with the children's. This made the writing of replies rather more difficult at first.

Les and Nigel's replies were sent to Anne for delivery. The children's reaction was very positive:

The replies from Les and Nigel came in a large envelope addressed to me. This was opened in front of the children and the individual letters were distributed. It is almost impossible for me to describe the atmosphere and sense of excitement as the children watched and waited. On previous occasions when 'envelopes' had been given out, it was usually because there was a child's birthday, or invitations to parties. At those times the children never knew if everyone was going to get one or only a select few. On this occasion, though, they knew that everyone was going to get a letter. For some children it seemed as if just getting the letter was excitement enough. I had to suggest to some that they actually read them. As most of the children were confident in themselves as readers, they showed no reluctance to read their letters unaided. It was clear, however, that not everyone understood them, and when children requested help, I read their letters with them. Some children set out to reply immediately; others put the letters in their work trays for working on later.

The letter writing exchange had well and truly begun. To be honest, none of us expected it to continue for very long. We were well aware of the volatility in young children's interests and the exchange was not a compulsory activity. Would it last a few weeks, a few months, a year?

This book covers the first two years of the letters but the exchange was nearing three years as the writing of the book ended. An interview with the children after two years revealed that they still enjoyed writing and receiving the letters, and that they wanted to continue without an end in view. One child commented, "We shall write till we're dead!"

Both Les and Nigel were aware of the commitment they had undertaken. Both accepted that, first and foremost, they were writing to the children because it was interesting to do so. Both also understood that, if they built up a personal relationship with the children through letters, they could not simply stop when they felt like it. They would continue to write until individual children indicated that they wished to discontinue the exchange, either directly or by ceasing to write. Both Les and Nigel now anticipate writing for many years to come.

Such a commitment brings problems, as Nigel found out.

It does take some time to write all the replies and it is not always easy to write a response that is unique to each individual. There have been two occasions when I departed from my good intentions. On one occasion, a bundle of letters arrived at the same time as about 80 very long assignments from my students. The assignments had to be graded as there was a crucial deadline involved. A rather long gap appeared in the correspondence. Then one day, this letter for me arrived at the polytechnic:

Dear nigel will you please
get a move on with your
Letter I have Been
wieting ages and ages
for you to rite me a
Letter I wish you
wuald hurry up if
you dont rite soon I
will never rite to you
a gian wot is hollding
you up
                    Love
                    From

**Needless to say, I replied straightaway. The letter had achieved
the intention of its author.**

It was only after the exchange of letters was well under way that
we really appreciated the kind of material we were getting from the
children. It became clear to us that, although we were primarily
writing to the children because it was an interesting and rewarding
thing to do, we were at the same time building up a unique set of data.
We decided to look at what was going on more systematically and to
collect other information which might help us to evaluate the nature
of the experience.

However, we were very concerned not to alter the essential
quality of the exchanges by adding this investigative dimension.
It was imperative that Nigel and Les continued to exchange letters
with the children because they were interested in what the children
had to say. They could not allow their letters to slide into something
manipulative. We believe the attempt to maintain the true nature
of the dialogue has been successful. The children in fact made it
easy for us by continuing to write interesting letters and to ask us
interesting questions.

The change to an investigatory project manifested itself in our
discussions about what was being written, in the closer examination
of the letters, and in the decision that Anne, as the non-letter writer,

would very occasionally and in a general way talk with the children about their letter writing. The only exception to this was when, after almost two years, each child, together with one of us, looked back at all the letters that had been exchanged.

Anne's classroom role continued to be as distributor, collector and sharer of the letters. The arrival of letters in the classroom continued to generate excitement and eagerness to learn what was in them, and the children went on sharing information with their friends. When a new batch of letters arrived, children could be seen quietly reading and occasionally showing something to a child next to them. Some children still needed a little help in reading their letters. This was sometimes provided by Anne but more often the child worked it out in conjunction with friends.

Inevitably, a number of incidents or changes took place during the two years, which affected the way the exchange operated. After only six months, for example, Les returned to the United States. This created a few problems for him:

> I realised when I got back to America that I had to establish another identity so as to be able to continue my personal dialogue with the children. I had to make the children aware of my life, where and how I lived, and what I did outside of my work. Doing this didn't seem easy and was complicated by the long gaps in receiving the letters, which often came by surface mail. In addition, once Anne had left the school, I had to rely on a new teacher who had not been in on the start of the project and didn't know me. Luckily, the headteacher was keen to ensure that the exchanges continued and was able to resolve any difficulties that occurred. Even she, however, could not stop a British postal strike that caused two sets of letters to arrive on the same day.

Les returned to England for a holiday almost two years after the exchanges started. This provoked an interesting situation. Through the letters both Les and Nigel had come to feel that they knew the children quite well. However, this was 'textually based' knowledge rather than face-to-face knowledge, and was as true for the children as it was for them. Les at first found it strange meeting with people he knew well by means of letters but not in person.

> I became a bit nervous about seeing the children, hoping I would recognise them and be able to relate to them. When Nigel and I walked in the room, we were welcomed with a great British "hip, hip, hooray" and I immediately felt better.
>
> Later, in talking with the children, I found some as open and responsive as they had been two years before; a few seemed more reserved and appeared to relate better through

writing than in oral communication. I was quite a stranger to them as a person and some of them may well have had difficulty reconciling memories of me and letter knowledge of me with my actual self. Generally, my knowledge of the children from their letters bridged the gap of time. Being able to ask about dance lessons, swimming, horseback riding, scouting, brothers and sisters was like meeting old friends after a period of separation.

Equally important were the changes that had taken place within the school. At the end of the first year of exchanges, the Local Education Authority determined that the school should lose one teacher. This necessitated some changes within the classes. The group of children that Anne had been teaching was split up. Some joined a slightly older group and some a slightly younger group. Most of Nigel's correspondents joined the older group. This had an interesting consequence for Nigel:

I was conscious that the long summer holiday posed problems for the letter writing exchange, so very early in the new term I wrote to every child in my group. At that time there were 12 of them in the new class. It was something of a shock to receive 25 letters in reply.

Although Nigel continued to correspond with all these children – and even acquired more – this book deals mainly with the letters from the children who started the exchange while in Anne's class. At the end of the following school year, the lost teaching position was restored and Anne's former class members were reunited.

Nigel was not the only person to acquire some additional correspondents. Les wrote to Anne and Nigel:

After the Christmas holiday, a letter arrived from an elder sister of one of the boys to whom I wrote. Then in the next exchange, another elder sister wrote. Soon some of their friends were writing.

Another change was Anne's return to her polytechnic lectureship. Of necessity, her contact with the children was reduced. However, she maintained a special link with the school and greatly facilitated the initiation of new teachers into the exchange.

During the full two-year period covered in the book, some children left the school. We debated whether to try to continue our correspondence with them and decided against it. We accepted as inevitable that our sample of children would grow smaller. We started with 30 children. Twenty of them have remained in the school and have continued without interruption as correspondents during the period of the exchanges. These are the children whose letters form the basis for this book.

Although these changes have necessitated some making-do, and have influenced the course of the exchanges, we do not see them in a negative way. The significant point is that the letters still go back and forth. Just as any correspondents go through changes in circumstances in their lives and situations, so our changes and difficulties had to be accepted as part of normal life in the real world.

All the children and their parents have been consulted about this book. We are sensitive that children often see their earlier work as inadequate, 'bad' or 'poor'. Children can be very critical of their earlier efforts. Although we ourselves view their early efforts as evidence of competence and success, we have, at the request of the children, used assumed names.

CHAPTER TWO

I howp youw can cum to schol qgeh

THE FIRST REPLIES

When starting a correspondence with someone, there is a very wide choice of topics. Somehow, a letter writer has to select those that they feel are the most appropriate. At the same time, cultures have established certain conventions in letter writing, and these conventions frequently influence some of the decisions about what is to go in a letter. This chapter is about the choices the children made when writing their first replies.

Each child was given a letter during the visit from Les and Nigel. Each letter was in an envelope with the child's name on it. All the letters were identical except that half were signed by Les and half by Nigel.

Dear

I have enjoyed being in your class. I hope you would like to write to me. I promise to write back to you

Love

The text of that letter had been chosen with care. We wanted it to contain an invitation to write back as well as a statement signalling enjoyment at having met the children. However, we were keen not to influence or predispose the children towards any particular topic for their reply. It was, in effect, a non-committal letter, friendly but vacuous. The responsibility for what to say in a reply was handed over to each child. Equally, each child was left to include or exclude any of the conventions associated with letter writing. The initial letter had been set out in a conventional form and was on headed notepaper but the children were given no further guidance or instructions about how their replies should be set out.

What do you say to someone you do not know well? What style do you adopt? What relationship do you assume? How do you choose to say it? Where do you pick your topics from? What do you think the other person wants to know? What assumptions do you make about a reply to your letter? Do you commit yourself to a relationship through the writing? The answers to these and other questions influence a response. They may not be answered explicitly but, in some way, each reply indicates a stance upon these questions. As we examined the children's letters, we were able to discover the possible assumptions made by the children in developing their replies. Their responses appeared to demonstrate four main strategies:

1 The 'reference to shared experience' strategy.

2 The 'I'll tell you all about me' strategy.

3 The 'I'll be your friend' strategy.

4 The 'I want to know more about you' strategy.

Of course, many of the letters contained elements of more than one of these strategies.

THE 'REFERENCE TO SHARED EXPERIENCE' STRATEGY

Letters written between friends often make great use of shared experience because this links people and gives them a common reference point. It is often a way of re-establishing the nature of a relationship. A lack of shared experience makes meaningful dialogue between two people very difficult. Only time and the existence of many exchanges gives a kind of shared experience which can then be drawn upon in future letters. The children, in writing their first replies, were faced with this problem. What kind of shared experience could give them a basis for the content of a letter? The strategy of many of them was to use the only bit of shared experience that did exist – the visit.

> Dear Nigel did yell LAke bee ihn ih myclss and hav
> you got Ani children yll wud you lnke to cum rrne Strawberry Fair

Did you like being in my class and have you got any children and would you like to come to the strawberry fair?

> Duar Les
> I have enjoyed your cumig to r
> Sohod I hope you would like to
> cume back from

I have enjoyed your coming to our school. I hope you would like to come back.

> Dear Nigel I hop you wul cum back to
> the school And my brether is
> B lyg gud And He is cod Danlel
> And He is8 Luv e from

I hope you will come back to the school. My brother is being good and he is called Daniel and he is 8.

Some children used the letter from Nigel and Les as a shared experience and, in doing so, began to approach one of the most natural conventions of letter writing, that of thanking the writer for their letter *(see over.)*

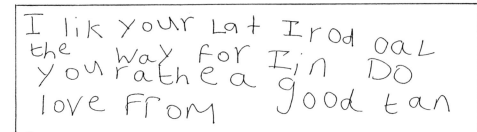

I like your letter. I read all the way through it. Did you have a good time?

One child made specific reference to the actual text of the letter from Nigel and Les, writing: "I have enjoyed you being in my class too". The word 'too' is significant. It clearly signals the picking up of a previous point and is a recognition of the dialogic nature of letter writing.

Both of these ways of using shared experience can be seen in many of the other first letters in this chapter.

THE 'I'LL TELL YOU ALL ABOUT ME' STRATEGY

The kind of information contained in letters of this type is perhaps what one might expect in the first letter to a penfriend. It reflects an understanding of the need of the audience to know more about the writer.

Dear Les
My name is Sue. and I have two sisters
my mum is called Ruth and my Dad is
called Denzel. my other sisters
are called Katy and Emily. my
favourite thing at home is playing
on the trampolinen. Love from Sue
X Y X X X X X X X X X X X X X X X X X X

MY SiSteR iS CQlled Alison
and She is fifteen and I
am Six and I am called
mary I donT liikt doing
PicTuRS and Tha Tis wy
I cant do a PicTuRe

It may also show awareness of the fact that, although Les and Nigel had visited the class and talked to many children, they really did not know very much about the children as individuals. Recognising that the reader needs, or would like, information about a new correspondent requires a mature level of social understanding.

The means chosen to represent this knowledge was the 'list'. Apart from being a contextually appropriate strategy, lists offer an entry into the world of coherent texts and, maybe, ultimately into the world of cohesive texts. Lists are coherent by virtue of being a collection of items. They do not have to be in any order. The lists in the letters above are collections of facts to do with each child's immediate family. These children were in part mapping their own world, but were doing so in the context of making their world comprehensible to other people. As such, their lists make perfect sense as maps of the most significant part of their world.

THE 'I'LL BE YOUR FRIEND' STRATEGY

Many of the letters expressed pleasure in the new-found relationship. Some were merely in the form of a wish for a return visit.

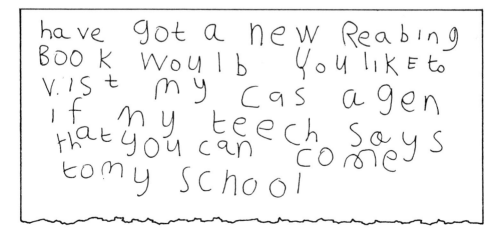

have got a new Reabing
Book woulb you likE to
V.iSt my cas agen
if my teech says
that you can come
tomy school

Dear Les
thank you For your Lett
I enJoyed you being in my class
and I have enjoyed nigel being
in my class as well I wish
you both could come again

class is vrey vrey vrey
noisey today when I
JuSt going to school was
Trapped my fingers I am 5
Love from

Others took this even further by inviting Nigel and Les to their homes.

Dear Nigel I have enJoyed
you bieing in my classtoo.
are you all rite and you can
come to my House oneday
love
x x x

One child extended an invitation to her birthday party even though it was 10 months off, and offered further enticement in the form of a description of the food.

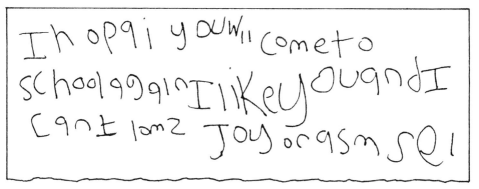

> Nigel Wud You Like to ...ymtomyparty we hc I a m7
> Nigel I MIt have a h Re o Jelly ahdI MIt
> have anchocolate cak a and Angeldelight

*Would you like to come to my party when I am 7? Nigel, I might have
red jelly and I might have a chocolate cake and angel delight.*

Some children presumed on the idea of friendship even further
and requested a visit to the homes of Nigel and Les.

> I h op9 i y ouw ll come to
> school 99 9in I like you an d I
> cant lom z Joy or 9sm se l

*I hope you will come to school again. I like you. Can I come to your
house, Nigel?*

Twenty-two out of the 30 children in some form or other expressed
the desire to extend the relationship or expressed pleasure in the relationship. For the most part this is done from the child's perspective
of making friends. The invitations are tokens of friendship: 'you are
my friend and you can come to tea'.

On one level, such responses may seem to be typically child-like:
children like extending invitations to other children to come to their
house. However, the fact that they have made these invitations to
two strange adults reflects an assumption of a social relationship.

It is perhaps important to note again that the children did respond
differently to Nigel and Les than they did to other adult visitors to
the classroom. For some reason they responded more like children
talking to adult friends of the family. In Les's case they were perhaps
more like grandchildren, with all respect to his youth. He had been
compared to one child's grandfather, who was known and liked
by most of the class. Their response in the letters was therefore a
reasonable response within their terms of reference, and altogether
appropriate.

THE 'I WANT TO KNOW MORE ABOUT YOU' STRATEGY

Having information about an individual is like having shared experience. It allows the writer to refer back to it or to draw on it in making hypotheses about a person. When a dialogue has not yet been established, the sensible way to gain such information is to ask questions. Quite a few of the children asked questions in their letters. Some used questions to clarify something about the visit.

Dear Nigel I have enJoyed you being at our school. When my grop Were in the plaY area did you really TaKe our Picture. Did you Like the house that we made my house is on willow road uPPermill. I have a little Brother called John he is three Years old. I am six years old my Sisters are 15 and 16 my mum and Dad are 42 and 39

Love from

Dear Mr Hall I hope You are well and I wood like your camera I love You To Write Back To Me What sort of camera i's it Big camera l6ts of love From

Some children asked questions to learn personal details.

I love yur letter
I like your house
Why ~~house~~ have hot you
got any chidren?

Dear Les weredo you work with peepul and is it fun.
do you have Sume frens. my op D Wou KS at manchester
my untee livs in manchester to She is cub anee
alis do you have a brutherlove from   XXXXXXXX.

Where do you work with people, and is it fun? Do you have some
friends? My dad works at Manchester. My auntie lives in Manchester
too. She is called auntie Alice. Do you have a brother?

The existence of questions in these letters is important in terms
of the child's conception of the exercise as dialogue. Why ask a
question unless you anticipate that the reader is going to reply? It
is clear that these children understood very well that they were
involved in a series of exchanges.

Conclusion
Although varied the first replies made by the children were anything but random. Every child seemed to be able to draw upon
previous experience or other people's experience, and to formulate
a hypothesis about what was appropriate for a letter. The children
also appeared able to utilise a variety of strategies within one letter
to give more power to the dialogic strength of the text. We are
convinced that the children wrote with care, thought, and sense.
Certainly Les and Nigel felt they had received letters which gave
them considerable scope for reply. In essence, the children had

made their job easier by laying foundations for future dialogue. It was also clear that the children understood that they had entered into some kind of sustained dialogue and that they wanted to be in that state. One child made this very clear.

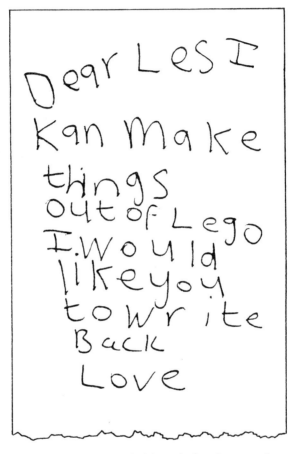

Dear Les I
Kan Make
things
out of Lego
I. would
like you
to write
Back
Love

The first replies from the children helped us understand some important points. It was clear that even inexperienced letter writers could make appropriate responses given a genuine letter writing context. All the children responded with a form and content that was appropriate to letter writing even though many did not contain all the conventions. Every child demonstrated that they understood that a genuine audience was going to read what they wrote. Every child employed strategies which recognised the dialogic nature of the communication, even though individuals used different strategies. They all anticipated a response to their letter and made it clear that they wanted to engage in the letter writing dialogue.

CHAPTER THREE

it w o svery nice to   Here your letter

DEVELOPMENT IN THE UNDERSTANDING AND USE OF SOME LETTER-WRITING CONVENTIONS

Conventions are highly significant social devices. Although they are arbitrary, each culture or group developing its own, at the same time they probably reflect deeper psychological needs. Conventions operate to regulate transactions between people; they operate as guidelines for behaviour. They have, nevertheless, evolved from custom and practice rather than been established as rule of law.

It is the existence of certain conventions that allow us to recognise easily a piece of text as belonging to the genre that is called 'letter writing'. Why do we put our address on a letter when we know that a recipient already knows it? Why do we put it in the top right-hand corner? Why do we put the date when it is often of no consequence? Why do we say 'Dear . . .' when we are writing to someone we hate or despise? What causes us to adopt the phrases: 'yours', 'yours faithfully', 'yours sincerely', 'yours affectionately', 'your most humble and obedient servant', 'love', 'many thanks'? Why do we normally indent the first line of a letter?

Leaving aside the more formal conventions, there are other, more subtle, conventions waiting within letters. After writing 'dear . . .' what does one say? Beginning and concluding letters is a bit like opening and closing conversations. We believe that entrance and exits within letters are equally complex and pose equally demanding problems for young letter writers.

In one sense, children have to learn that there is an issue at all. After all, why not simply start with what you want to say and stop when you have written it. Identifying the issue demands some kind of social, and consequently, contextual sense: a realisation that your communication is to a person with whom you have a relationship that involves more than just passing messages.

In order to examine how the children in our group developed understandings of convention, we have divided the conventions into those which we see as more formal: date, address, salutation, and closure, and those which we see as carrying a more intellectual load: the beginning and ending of the main text.

THE FORMAL CONVENTIONS

We are fairly confident from conversations with the children and discussions with many of the parents that, when the letter-writing exchange began, the children had little experience of writing letters. Thus the children's responses to our initial letter were inevitably going to be based on very limited experience of letter writing.

The first letters

We have 30 first letters from the children. Subsequently, during the two years of the exchanges we lost 10 children from the group. In this chapter, when dealing specifically and solely with the first letters, we have drawn from all 30 of them. Other analyses or illustrations in this book are from the 20 children who have been in continuous correspondence.

The address and date   Ten children simply put the name of the school, 13 put the full address and nine put the date.

Salutation   All the children except one started their letter with either 'Dear Les' or 'Dear Nigel'.

Closure   Twenty-four of the children signed off with 'love', three simply put 'from', and three put nothing. Only two children failed to put their names on their letters; these same two also omitted any address and date.

Layout   Only two children laid their letters out in a conventional way. However, 17 of the children made a very good attempt and failed mainly by not separating the salutation or closure from the body of the text. Eleven children used a format which owed little to convention.

In order to consider changes in the children's ability to use the more formal conventions of letters, we will briefly consider the fifth and the tenth letters. We will not consider salutations further because use of this convention was so universal.

The fifth letters

Address and date   After the initial success in using the address and date, there was a considerable drop-off. By the fifth letter, only five children gave partial addresses and none gave a full address. Six gave a date. We suspect that the children were much more involved with the business of actually saying something. Form, in other words, became much less important than content.

Closure   Almost all the children closed with 'love' and did so from then on. Therefore we will not consider this category again.

Layout   Only one child had a complete conventional layout and eleven were close. Allowing for the omission of children who had left, these figures are about the same as for the first letters.

The main difference between these and the first letters was the use of illustrative material either in the form of pictures or patterns. Thirteen of the children drew pictures or patterns with their letters.

The tenth letters

Address and date   Twelve out of the 20 gave a complete address and 18 gave the date. By this time the children had a new teacher and clearly there had been some discussion about the use of addresses and dates. What is significant is that a move towards using the date and full address caused no problems at all for the children at this stage of the exchange. If these conventions had been introduced in a more formal way earlier, when the letters were very short, we suspect that it would have interfered with the children's willingness to develop the content. There is little joy to a child in having to write a date and address when doing so takes as much time and space as the content of the letter.

Layout   Eleven children were now using a fully conventional layout. Only one was still very unclear.

Like the first letters, there was no illustrative material in these letters. On the whole, the children have used very few illustrations in their letters, although there was a period when quite a number put patterns around their letters. At no time were the children told not to put illustrations. Indeed, Nigel tried on a number of occasions to encourage his correspondents to do so. It is as if the children had come to the conclusion that letters were for written text rather than drawing.

BEGINNING AND ENDINGS

As indicated above, we believe that beginnings and endings carry a significantly greater cognitive load than do many of the other conventions of letter writing. However, we suspect that beginnings pose fewer difficulties for young children than do endings.

'Beginnings' is a somewhat ambiguous term, even when the salutation is left aside. The opening unit of most letters, which is part of a sequence, is a stylised, conventional sentence which thanks the writer for their letter. Virtually every letter to the children from Les and Nigel began with such a sentence, although both went to some pains to vary it in minor ways. Such opening comments, although used fairly unreflectively by most letter writers, nevertheless serve a dialogic function in that they pick up on the preceding part of the dialogue, although not in specific form. We will now look at the first sentences of the children but we will also consider a few of the sentences that follow them. To begin a letter with 'Many thanks for your letter' certainly opens it in a physical sense; however, it still leaves the difficulty of selecting how to go on to the message part of the letter.

An examination of all the letters written to Nigel by seven girls shows that at first there was only one letter that began with:

I like your letter.

By the third letter there were two such openings and by the fifth there were four such openings:

Thank you for the postcard.

I loved your letter.

I like the butterfly very much. (A reference to the postcard.)

Thank you for your letter.

By the tenth letter every girl who wrote to Nigel opened with a 'thank you'. Although the openings followed an underlying pattern, there was quite a bit of minor variation in the surface pattern. Sometimes the use of such a phrase was unreflective. For example, one of the children started with *'Thank you for the letter, I liked it very much'*, when she had not in fact received a letter since the last one she wrote. Others were more aware than that, saying:

Thank you for your letter but I have lost it.

I can't say thank you for the letter cos I haven't got a letter.

I was hoping that you would send me a letter.

As indicated in chapter 1, there were times when the absence of a letter from either Les and Nigel stimulated a vigorous opening, which certainly reminded Les and Nigel of their obligations as correspondents:

Will you please get a move on, if you don't we won't write to you.

I did not get a letter from you.

Will you please get a move on with your letter.

Some clearly took the opening, although ritualised, as an opportunity for going further into the letter:

Thank you for your letter. It was very nice. I keep all the letters I get from you in a folder.

Thank you for the letter. I was away when Mrs Magson read out the letter so I listened to it again because there was quite a few of us so Rebecca read it out and it was very nice to hear such a long letter.

And some used the opening lines to apologise:

Dear Nigel, Thank you for your letter. Next time I will send it quicker.

The fact that the children only gradually moved towards the use of the ritualised 'thank you for your letter' meant that they had to be using some other strategy for starting. The strategy adopted by most was to pick up on one of the questions or main features of the previous letter to them. Les and Nigel tried to avoid using too many questions so that the letters would not become too much like a typical teacher–pupil dialogue. However, it would be pretty unnatural for letters between friends to contain no questions. Indeed, when tried, it proved very hard to write letters with no questions.

The children did seem to pay some attention to the models provided by Les and Nigel's letters, as this sequence of openings shows:

Child *Thank you for the postcard.*

Nigel *Wow what a long letter.*

Child *Thank you for the long letter you wrote me. I think it is a very long letter.*

Nigel *Thank you for your lovely letter.*

Child *Thank you for your lovely letter.*

Nigel *Thank you for your interesting letter.*

Child *Thank you for your long letter.*

Child *I went to a party yesterday.*

This sequence begins with the girl thanking Nigel for a postcard. His comment on the length of her letter in response is picked up and used in the child's next letter. When Nigel then uses 'lovely', it is also picked up in the succeeding letter. The word 'interesting' is not and the girl continues to use 'long'. Significantly when the seventh letter did not get a reply and the girl had to find another opening, she selected one which takes her straight into an interesting event. It would certainly seem that this child was sensitive to the openings that Nigel was using but not so unreflectively as to include a conventional opening when it was inappropriate. Although the relationships between Les and Nigel's openings and those of the children are not usually as clear as the example above, Les and Nigel felt that echoes of their openings appeared in the children's letters on many occasions.

35

Conclusions appear to be more problematic than beginnings as there seem to be fewer obvious conventions available. Indeed, the problem of concluding a letter is the problem of drawing a text to a point where it can be left without either strain to the text or the relationship. What counts as satisfactory will be very much a function of the context of the whole letter and the nature of the dialogic relationship that exists between the letter writers. The children, despite the cognitive difficulty of achieving such conclusions, in many different ways did show sensitivity to the need for some kind of genuine ending.

Nigel and Les usually concluded their letters with some invocation to write back to them:

You must write and tell me all about it.

I shall look forward to hearing from you.

Do write and let me know about what you are doing.

These very conventional endings were in fact seldom used by the children. There are relatively few examples where a child has finished with a similar expression. However, some have on occasion clearly adopted the model offered by Les and Nigel. From the second exchange onwards, a few of the children acknowledged the dialogic nature of the letter writing by closing with a request for a continuation:

I hope you will write back.

Please will you write back.

I love getting letters too.

Please answer me and write to me soon.

Most of the children may have felt, as Les and Nigel came to feel, that it was a fairly facile way to end a letter when you were pretty certain that a reply was going to follow anyway. Both Nigel and Les now try to avoid using these types of phrases.

The children seemed to be able to adopt a variety of strategies for concluding a letter, and each child used a whole range of such strategies.

A large number of the children's letters simply came to an end when the child decided to stop:

I have drawn something for you.

We watch the A Team it is good.

In the box there was some ducklings they were very nice and soft.

Many times these endings were conclusions in their own right, but to be seen as such need to be considered in the context of a larger portion of the letter:

The book week has started and we started it by doing a play, and I will tell you all about it. First we started with Mrs Robinson saying, 'Today we are doing a play', and Mrs Robinson said 'give me a "B", give me an "O", give me another "O", give me a "K" and what have we got, "BOOKS"'. And then some people did characters but I did not have a character but I had a book. At the end we showed the postcard and at the end of the assembly Mrs Magson told us to leave.

it is Mothers day on Sunday
13th March and I am giving my mum three
lots of stuf one from school and one from my club
I go to it on Tuesday so it will be on
to night and a bov of Cherys all Gold and
and three cards all From me to my mum

In these two examples, the final sentence is the end of a topic, although maybe not a typical letter ending. It draws the episode to an end and seems to be a natural ending for the letter. Although unconventional, it works as a strategy because the reader feels a sense of completeness.

Of course, these young letter writers, just like all letter writers, sometimes forget to mention things in their letter until they reread what they had written; or they reread the previous letter to them and realised that they had not answered a question; or they were not prepared to answer any more questions, even though they had noticed them:

Oh I forgot something in the Christmas presents I got a book as well.

Yes I do know where Brussels is its the capital of Belgium isn't it?

I answered a lot of questions in another letter.

Sometimes the children acknowledged the dialogic nature of the exchange by concluding with a question:

Do you know I go to swimming club?

Have you heard of Swallows and Amazons books?

And would you like to come to a dressing-up party?

What did you get for Christmas?

Some children became aware that they sometimes needed a way of getting out of writing more without appearing too abrupt:

I cannot tell you anything else that is about my holiday so I will say goodbye.

I can't think of anything else to say.

I'm sorry that I have to go now, I am looking forward to your coming.

Sorry I can't tell you any more.

I don't know what else I can tell you so lots of love.

I can't remember what else I did.

Others used some quite sophisticated endings:

Are you keeping in touch with Les? Is he keeping in touch with you? Keep well.

Do you know Les's address because I thought it would be good if I could write to you at school and write to Les at home.

I will write to you at home. Do you know my address? I don't know yours.

A few children were able to employ a conventional strategy when writing a letter to someone about to go on a long journey:

I am glad you are going to Arizona. I hope you have a good time.

I hope you have a nice train journey.

Anyway, I hope you enjoy it in Arizona.

The 'anyway' in the last example is a good demonstration of sensitivity to the need for some kind of device to draw a letter to a close.

The fact that the children did not use a consistent way of ending is not an example of inadequacy but a powerful argument for their sensitivity to the text that they had constructed. When the letters are examined, the endings are frequently ones that are contextually appropriate. It was Les and Nigel who disregarded textual appropriateness and resorted to using convention in a fairly unreflective way.

Conclusion

Our examination of the correspondence indicates that these young children had little difficulty in using the convensions of letter writing. Most of the children were able to employ a variety of strategies to begin and to end a letter. It was clear that many of these strategies implicitly acknowledged the dialogic nature of letter writing, and that their use of those strategies was sensitive to the textual and contextual demands of the individual exchanges.

CHAPTER FOUR

but I wish I knew what that scratching noise was.

DEVELOPING AS LETTER WRITERS

The large number of letters between the children and each of their correspondents makes it impossible for us to give anything other than a glimpse of the exchanges. Even to reproduce in full one set of the correspondence would take up more space than we can allot. However, wanting to give some sense of how the children developed as letter writers, we are going to look at a sample of the letters from two boys and two girls. Two of these children found writing relatively easy and two found it more of a problem.

All the exchanges are between Nigel and the children. We have not chosen Nigel's because his letters are different, more significant or better than Les's. The reason is a more pragmatic one. Because of the distance and problems with postage on letters to Les, there are fewer exchanges between him and his group of correspondents. In order to give the widest possible perspective on the children's development, we have elected to look at the group for whom we have the greatest number of letters.

In examining the letters as exchanges, it is necessary to consider what Nigel wrote. However, to save space we have had to make do with occasional quotes from Nigel's letters, and sometimes a simple comment. (For examples of full letters from Nigel and Les, see the Appendix.)

Each child is considered separately. The letters come from three periods. For each child we have reproduced the first five letters of the exchanges. The next sample comes from exchanges between June 1987 and about November 1988. The final group of extracts come from the exchanges which took place as the two-year period came to an end.

Our concern throughout the book, but especially in this chapter, is to look at the children as letter writers. For that reason, the bulk of our comments concern features which we feel are special to letter writing.

In considering the children as letter writers, we focus principally on features which identify the exchange as a partnership. We will be looking for evidence of a willingness to provide information, to seek information, to maintain the friendly relationship, and to embed what they write about within the context of increasingly shared experience of each other. We will also be looking to see how children respond to the topics generated by their correspondent and to discover the extent to which the children are influenced by, and are able to influence, the topics selected by their correspondent.

A letter exchange represents a form of dialogue. However, as dialogue it is very different from that of conversation. For our purposes, dialogue means the written exchanges necessary to maintain and develop the social relationships across time and space between the writers. If topics or themes are pursued across letters, then the continuity of that dialogue becomes stronger; that in turn has implications for the social relationship. Although the exchanges were not frequent, they were on the whole regular. On average during the two years an exchange occurred every fortnight. Thus each child would write and receive one letter a month.

The children featured in this chapter were very young. They were between five and a half and six-years-old when the exchanges began. It is in this context that our admiration of their abilities must be considered.

MARK

Mark was already a capable and confident writer when the exchange began and his first reply was very clearly recognisable as a letter. It contained two topics. The first was a reference to himself, part of the 'I'll tell you all about me strategy', and the second sought to extend the relationship between the writers through a question. From the start, Mark seemed aware of some of the obligations of being a participant in letter exchange.

> Dear Nigel thank you for the Letter I got from you I am in class 2 and I work very hard. Would you come to my house one day

Mark's selection of subject was seized upon by Nigel who referred to it but also developed it by extending the topic into writing stories.

I was pleased to hear that you work very hard. What kind of work do you like best? Do you like writing? I like writing stories. Perhaps I will send one of my stories to Mrs Robinson and she can read it to you.

Dear nigel some day You will No all about me and I will give You a bookToo. Do You no all abour me and Will You write and Would You write to me. on Friday We goiN The play area. Whenl ris saritday I watch NUmBer 73. I Like writing about you When are You goiNg to give me the book.

Some day you will no all about me and I will give you a book, too. Do you no all about me and will you write and would you write to me? On Friday we are going in the play area. When it is Saturday I watch Number 73. I like writing about you. When are you going to give me the book?

Mark's opening statement provided us with an apt title for the book. It encapsulated the very essence of a letter-writing dialogue: a growth in a relationship between two people. His second sentence was, in effect, a challenge to Nigel: do you really mean what you said about writing to me? He clearly homed in on the notion of the book as a personal gift to him. He was, in essence, staking a claim which Nigel had to address in some way. In his reply, Nigel took up Mark's notion of the book but the wording of his letter was somewhat ambiguous with respect to Mark's original interpretation of the offer.

I am going to try and find one of my stories for you. It is about a boy who went to the zoo to try and teach the animals to read and write. Do you think he was silly? I wonder if animals can read and write? I know my snakes cannot read or write.

In his next letter Mark tried a new opening, which could be polite convention or a genuine request about Nigel's health. Whichever it was, it provided a link with the previous letter as it led on to an enquiry about the health of the snakes. The reference to a sister and the goldfish seem somewhat out of context in the dialogue until one realises that these were a reflection of the way in which the children had been sharing their letters with each other.

Dear Nigel I hope You are well are
Your snakes well I bet Your
sister is 14 how old are You are
You 14 too. have You flushed the
gold Fish Down the toilet yet. when the
are you going to sned a book to me
Nigel. on Friday is my Favourite me Day
green group goes in the Playarea.

By coincidence, the snakes had not been well when Nigel replied and he was able to extend the theme. The promised book was finally sent to be shared with the class and Mark's response to it was requested.

Dear Nigel I liked the story that
You sent me. What kind
OF medicine did You give Your
snakes was it snake medicine
I am going To
are You going get a Easter egg
egg togeto Easter

In thanking Nigel for the book, Mark appeared to have effectively terminated this topic and we wonder whether the use of an exceptionally large full stop was a sign of the firmness of the closure. The letter reflected a variety of strategies as he looked back, provided new input and concluded with a question which generated a new topic.

It was after Easter when Nigel replied but he picked up on the topic introduced by Mark.

Did you get some Easter eggs? I didn't get any. But I did go out on several days. Les and I went to Lincoln which is a very old city.

A postcard, enclosed with the letter, added colour and variety to the dialogue. Mark's reply was an unusual one.

I hankyou For a Post card.
I Like the castle.
What are your Snakes called
Who do you like best.
What do you do. do you like
that Book What you sent
me. do you like it Best
Do you Write letters

Clearly the book topic had not been completely closed. However, Mark's use of questions is the most significant feature of this letter. While he had asked questions before, most of this letter consists of questions to which he already knew the answers. It seems as if he were experimenting with the question technique. In doing so, he did not show the same balance or variety as in previous letters.

Mark was by now well into the routine of being a letter writer. He seemed to have a clear idea of what was needed to maintain the dialogue and what was needed to extend it. For him, growth consisted of being able to exercise more control over his writing in such ways that his purposes as a letter writer were more easily met.

During the middle period his letters grew considerably longer. For example, one year after his first letter of 27 words, he was writing letters of around 200 words. As his capability to write at length developed, so did the problem of what to say and how to organise it.

Dear Nigel
        Thank you for giving me a nice letter.
I write to my grandma in oldham and nickles who is my cousin.
how many people do you write to in hong kong? why dont you
put three words in hong kong and how many people do yo now in
america and australia? have you ever seen blue peter because
it shouded the teracoter armary and it shouded how to make
you very own folder how many people have you writen
to in a full week? I have writen to ten people in one
day but they got lost in the post xxx
It is my birthday on feb 19th
PS please send a   Love
Present   from

Unlike his letter of the previous year, when he experimented with questions to which he already knew the answers, this letter shows his developing maturity. His questions, although persistent, ask for information he did not have. He did not need to experiment with questions any more. He now used them as a normal part of dialogic exchange. He was able to use questions in a somewhat rhetorical way. They existed as a device which allowed him to make a comment. In his reply, Nigel picked up on some of Mark's questions but began his letter by saying:

Thank you for your lovely letter. I guess I have missed your birthday. All your letters didn't arrive until last week. I hope you had a lovely birthday and got loads of presents.

Mark responded with one of his longest letters and used it to extend the topic of his birthday *(see over)*.

Dear Nigel

thankyou for giving me you nice letter I had did have a party. I had fifteen people coming. I had fiften presents on my birthday I got a baby gloworm and sally gave me a Ladybird it was a pencil howlder and the eyes were rubbers grace gave me some choclates they wer rosas they have some of the milk tray and some other kinds they are wrapped in couloured paper. we played Lots of nice games and we got changed into nice clothes and a magison came and did some magic and emma had a Leaving party and a magisan came to the place were claire my sister use to go dancing. I made a book about my birthday and it is called the birthday and it is not a big one at school It is my own book and It is a good one.

The shift towards greater control of the text was very marked in that letter. Most of the letter was a sustained account of his birthday and followed the sequence of events. Mark's understanding of the need to satisfy his audience was orchestrated with his growing ability to use written language. The result was a more satisfying and complete recount. This was a significant shift from his earlier letters when a cluttered sample of topics would appear in apparently random order. The letter was still list-like but the sequence was appropriate and sustained.

The recognition that writers have obligations towards their correspondent in terms of giving complete accounts and in presenting information in a way that could be followed easily can cause tension for a young letter writer. The next letter is a wonderful example of what can happen when personal interest meets social obligation.

Dear Nigel

I liked the very long letter and I had a go on a two weeler bike and I have never had a go I couldn't ride a two weeler bike and I had a try and I did it I am going on holiday to meyorca and I am going on a plane I like racheal and I might call for her. Racheal let me have a go on her bike and it is not steady and we made these litte thing's and they are made of paper. I have made a dragon and fish. I am on Sandwitches and I was on it before grace and I am still on Sandwitches and I like ham best of all and I am going to get a bike for christmas

As a more mature writer, he may have recognised that he needed to do more than inflict his obsessions upon his correspondent but he could not avoid constant return to what for him was a burning interest. The reference to Rachel appeared initially to be a new topic, but no. Mark reveals that it was just a strategy for persisting with his pressing interest in a two-wheeler bike.

As Mark moved towards the end of the first two year's correspondence he introduced a new genre into his letters and used, for the first time in the correspondence, a cognitive verb. He was proficient in using the affective verb formulations but now here appears 'I think' (see over).

Dear Nigel
Thank you for your letter
I think you should go and See
the lights. I have Some friends
in Black Pool. I did not go up
to the top. of tower.   I
have Seen Some tortoises before
I will right a little Story for you
about a tortoise

tortoise meets a dragon

one day a tortoise was was walking in
the wood and he fownd that something
green fell on him

it was a dragon. he had fownd a friend
then they had a Shower. it fluded the
house then they learned to Swim

then the dragon opened the door
and the flood went out and then
they tidyed the house and then
they had there tea and went to
bed.

The introduction of a story was unusual, not only for Mark but for any of the children. At the beginning of this letter he was responding to a fairly detailed discussion in Nigel's letter about the illuminations at Blackpool. This done, he seemed to be at a loss for something to write. It may be significant that this letter was written in cursive script to start with, something the children were beginning to learn at school. Was it the stress of having to write in this way which led him to search for something easy with which to complete his letter, or did he simply not have anything more to say but felt that his obligations as a correspondent dictated that there should be more? Whatever the reason, he then switched back to printing for the story.

Nigel replied to Mark but a delay at the school meant that there was no reply from Mark before Christmas. Nigel wrote again immediately after Christmas to pick up the exchange. He asked no questions, which meant that Mark had to generate his own topics *(see over)*.

I have not written to you for a long time. We have been to the Saddleworth museum and we saw some motor cars and motor bikes and a Penny fathing. when we came back we did a Poom about car bikes lorry and Vans. We are going to go ro Granada on the 17th of Febuary and that is two days before my birthday.

Friday 3rd Febuary

we are going to be making some biscuits and we are going to go to make a packet for them we are going to make an advert about them I am nearly eight. David is the oldest in our class. Justin is the youngest in our class. helen is just one day younger than david. Ben is just ten days older than me.

School-based events formed the focus of his letter which was written at two different times. His report of the visit to the museum makes an interesting contrast with that of Matthew, which follows. Mark's account was objective, precise and sequential, but restricted to a straightforward description of what was seen. Matthew by contrast offered a perspective on what he had seen.

In his response, Nigel picked up on most of the points made by Mark but spent more time dealing with the class visit to Granada TV and the biscuit making.

> **I am glad you enjoyed your visit to Granada. You must tell me all about it. I have not been there so I don't know anything about it . . . How did the biscuits come out? I have never tried to make biscuits. I like cooking very much but avoid making things like cakes and biscuits. They are too difficult for me.**

Mark responded to these points in what was quite a complex letter (*see over*).

I hope you are well. we have got a new boy he is called Shawn. He is a very nice boy. It is nearly easter. I might not get any easter eggs. we have been to granada and it was good. Do you still have your snakes which do you think are strongest Peter Claire's budgie and your snakes I would think you snakes would win. what are you going to do in the easter holidays I am going to go to butlins I think it might be nice. I like monday because it is P. E. lesson and I like the trapeze best. when you were travel -ing half way round the world did you have different times on clocks cos I have Just got your letter Friday 7 march the biscuts turned out to be nice and we made a picture

of the bisuits but I have not done one but some other. People. when we were there we saw the Granada ghost we went up these stairs and they lit up. when we went to the Thearte workshop and there was a victorian school and there was a spelling test we had to read words.

In this final example of Mark's letters, we can see a much more reflective and expressive style, contrasting markedly with his previous letter. But it is the range of strategies which make this a more impressive example of letter writing. He maintained the relationship through the opening greeting, picked up on topics raised by Nigel, responded to questions, added further explicit comment and provided unsolicited information with more detailed explanation. Embedded in the middle of the letter was his unusual question about the animals. That question picked up on an important aspect of an ongoing correspondence, the use of reference back to letters from some time ago. The snakes were last mentioned in the fifth letter and Claire's budgerigar was named in the tenth. Mark could use both these references with confidence because he knew that, for the two correspondents, this represented shared experience.

By now Mark was a very fluent writer. He had good command of a range of strategies and was a committed, equal partner in the exchange. He was able to produce fairly well balanced and coherent letters. He provided information, responded to his reader's enquiries, was not afraid to make demands upon his correspondent, and maintained the social relationship through regular comments which expressed satisfaction or friendliness. The later letters used more indirect and interrelated strategies than the direct and discontinuous moves of earlier letters. Mark had developed into a very confident and capable letter writer.

MATTHEW

Even a casual inspection of Matthew's letters will show that the mere act of making marks on paper demanded considerable effort. However, despite this difficulty, Matthew was never a reluctant author and was always an enthusiastic participant in the exchanges with Nigel. Like all the children, Matthew's letters were highly individual: they represented a voice which was his and could be no-one else's.

Matthew started at a disadvantage. He was absent when Les and Nigel visited the school and gave out the initial letters. He therefore had no direct knowledge of Les and Nigel, no invitation to write, and little knowledge of the context within which the exchange was to take place. Matthew did not want to be excluded from the exchange and was very aware that, as far as the rest of the children were concerned, something very interesting was taking place in the classroom. He elected to write to Nigel. With what we would term an acute sense of audience, he clarified his position to his correspondent.

*I was not at school when you came and I was at home when you came.
My friend Martin told me about your two snakes.*

While the text had no punctuation, no spaces between the words, temporary spelling, and poor letter formation, it was nevertheless a letter – a very short but reasonable letter. He made his points clearly, signified his interest and showed that he considered himself a worthy correspondent not to be left out.

Nigel responded to Matthew's letter by describing himself and asking for a description in return.

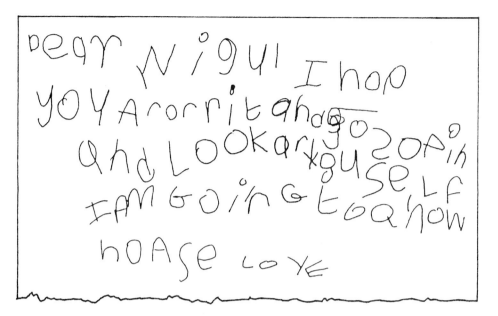

I hope you are all right and looking after yourself. I am going to a new house.

Matthew ignored Nigel's request but offered a new topic. Nigel used that topic in his reply. He picked up on the forthcoming Easter holidays and maintained the talk about the new house *(see over)*.

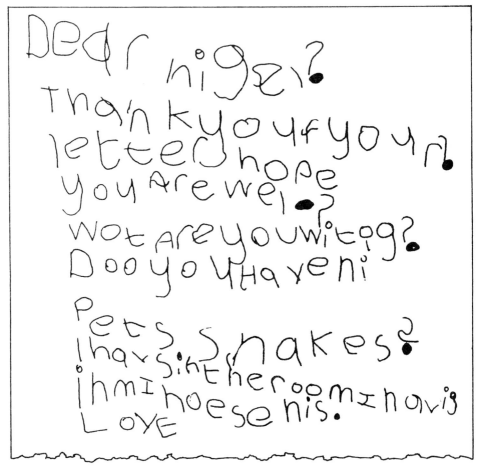

Thank you for your letter. I hope you are well. What are you writing?
Do you have any pet snakes? I have seen the room I am having in my
new house.

This letter started, as did his previous one, with a conventional, relationship-maintaining strategy. It was something relatively few of the children did at this point in the exchanges. He had obviously discovered question marks but, in common with many children who are fascinated by this punctuation mark, applied it incorrectly. This piece was the work of a confident author even though it may not have been the work of a confident handwriter or speller. It was vigorous and he was not afraid to tackle conventions, to interrogate his correspondent, or to maintain his themes. The dialogue about the house, although somewhat lacking in cohesion, continued.

Nigel wrote after the Easter break, explaining how he had spent Easter and sending Matthew (and every child) a postcard relating to part of his holiday. Matthew picked up Nigel's theme.

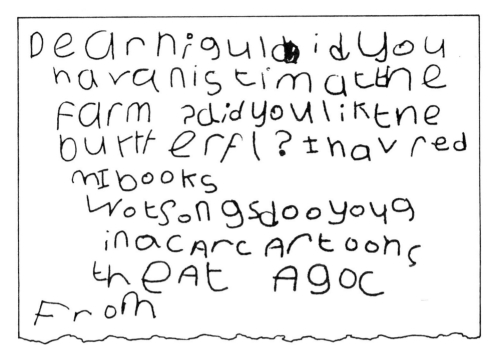

Did you have a nice time at the farm? Did you like the butterflies? I have read my books. What song do you sing in a car? Cartoons. That is a joke . . .

Matthew maintained the social relationship through his questions. The inclusion of a joke in this letter was certainly unusual in the children's letters. Once again Matthew's determination to be his own person produced something interesting, a different genre within a letter.

Despite Nigel offering a joke in his reply, Matthew ignored it and introduced new topics in his fifth letter *(see over)*.

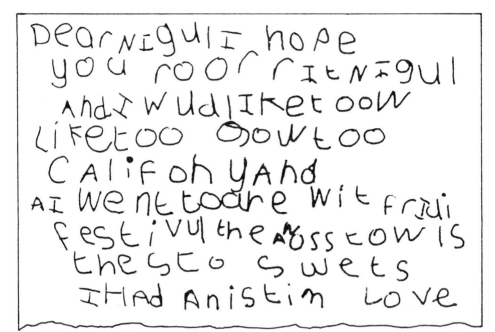

I hope you are alright, Nigel and I would like to go to California. I went to the Whit Friday Festival. There was stalls. The stalls sell sweets. I had a nice time.

In the fifth letter Matthew not only picked a topic for the first time but also extended it with brief additional detail. He extended the context for his reader.

These early exchanges showed Matthew as a writer in control of his own voice. He was not playing second fiddle to Nigel's greater competence as a writer; he was a correspondent whose voice would be heard. While the dialogue may not have been strong, the consistent use of relationship-maintaining devices kept the correspondence going.

When Nigel wrote at the beginning of the new school year to enquire how Matthew liked his new class, Nigel also said:

I am going to America to see Les. I am going in an aeroplane. The journey is going to take 22 hours as I have to change planes several times.

Matthew responded:

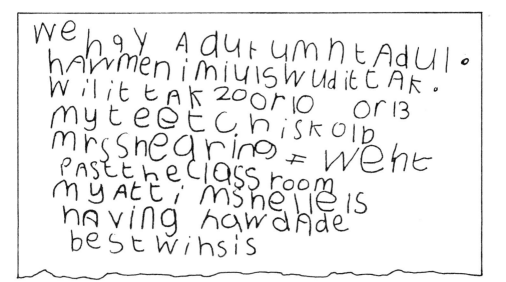

We have an Autumn table. How many miles would it take? Will it take 20, or 10 or 13? My teacher is called Mrs Shearing. I went past the classroom. My Auntie Michelle is having a baby.

Matthew questioned Nigel about the distance to America. The content of the question was quite reasonable given the information about how long it will take to get there. At the same time, it revealed the naivety of his concepts about distance.

One of Matthew's comments demands further explanation. "I went past the classroom" is a response to Nigel's question about Matthew's new classroom. On his first day back, Matthew was so unfamiliar with his new terrain that he walked right past the new classroom. Matthew's failure to contextualise this comment makes great demands on his reader.

The first shift of this period began to emerge around the tenth and eleventh letters. In his reply to Matthew's ninth letter, Nigel had asked about the new cafeteria system at the school *(see over)*.

thank you for your letter I like camtin
scaIt and thundberds and
Stingray wote doo you like?
I like in the caffa taerea crisps
I play on my Bmx it gos fasj
I play witn my wib

Thank you for your letter. I like Captain Scarlet and Thunderbirds and Stingray. Who do you like? I like crisps in the cafeteria. I play on my BMX bike. It goes fast. I play with my whip.

Nigel chose to follow up the reference to the TV puppets.

Thank you for telling me you like Captain Scarlet and Thunderbirds. I have never seen it. Perhaps you can write and tell me all about it – then I will know what I am missing. You asked me what I like to watch. I suppose I like all the programmes about animals and plants.

thak you for your letter in Stingray they fite and kill
and runaway. andI have a pet dog Called max
and a gole fish I had a red nose on comic rief
day I woch TV all the time I woch
tickul on the tum
inThunddrads they hit ech uth

Thank you for your letter. In Stingray they fight and kill and run away. And I have a pet dog called Max and a goldfish. I had a red nose on Comic Relief day. I watch TV all the time. I watch Tickle on the Tum. In Thunderbirds they hit each other.

In this more extended response, Matthew stuck fairly well to the TV theme. He actually answered Nigel's question, but for only the second time in his letters, also offered extra information. It may seem a small move but it was a significant one as such expansions occurred with greater frequency from then on. The exchanges were becoming more dialogic.

Towards the end of the school year Nigel wrote a very long communal letter to the class, giving details of his forthcoming trip to Australia. He ended by saying:

It will soon be your Summer holidays. I expect that many of you are going to interesting or even unusual places. When I come back you will have to write and tell me all about your Summer holidays.

Matthew's next two letters can be seen as one sustained response, even though one was written before the holiday and one after.

What are you doing? Are you going to Canada? I am going to Portsmouth on Saturday. We are staying in a caravan. We are back now. It is 200 [miles] to Portsmouth. In Hong Kong do you know the language? Is it good?

I have bine to saw th Sae
the capital of Potsmoth
this boat coald Gotland
cam in and we saw the
Qeen alizadath and it was
Good in Hong Kong is
ther trams I hope you
hav a nis time

I have been to Southsea, the capital of Portsmouth. This boat called Gotland came in and we saw the Queen Elizabeth and it was good. In Hong Kong are there trams? I hope you have a nice time.

Matthew was still writing short letters but they were developing thematically, as both the above letters show. The topic was maintained across almost the whole of the letters. This was another major shift for Matthew as it offered the reader much greater contextualisation of the topics.

The apparent simplicity of Matthew's letters during the year of this second period should not distract from the positive elements within them or the fact that some significant changes took place. His letters revealed a child asking and answering questions, maintaining the relationship through positive affirmation, expressing likes and dislikes, and providing new topics for his reader.

Towards the end of the second year of writing, Matthew's letters began to show more obvious signs of development. In his first letter of the new year, he responded to earlier questions of Nigel's about school.

Dear Nigel I went too Birmingham on Sunday. I crast on my go kart. I have got droose we have made some maps old Wonse we drowd it frst and then we wragt id abot it wich I have bene doing. we have de to the muesem to have a look at the Old fasha Cars and fire enges it was good it was uppremill muesem my pantern was Ben morton martin my Best frend werct with me and the fire was the dest I dm ok yes Scool is boring I am ingoy my self. woke is d boring. I have a istrmt I dm get in a nuoo wan to hige. it is a baritoh

from

I went to Birmingham on Sunday. I crashed my go-cart. I have got a bruise. We have made some maps, old ones. We drew it first and then we wrote about it, which I have been doing. We have been to the museum to have a look at the old fashioned cars and fire engines. It was good. It was Uppermill museum. My partner was Ben Morten. Martin, my best friend, walked with me. The fire engine was the best. I am OK. Yes school is boring. I am enjoying myself. Work is boring. I have an instrument. I am getting a new one tonight. It is a baritone.

The most obvious feature of this letter was its length. It was 113 words long and about twice as long as his longest previous effort. As with all writers, once he could write more he had to face up to the issue of organising his text. Matthew managed this very effectively. After a brief factual statement about his visit and accident he concentrated on school-related issues. In doing so, he was providing an extended response to Nigel's question about school. The material was organised very effectively. Related topics were grouped together and there was an awareness of his reader's need for detail.

Matthew provided Nigel with a wealth of material on which to comment. The whole of Nigel's reply was taken up by responses to the points Matthew had made. So Matthew much more effectively influenced his correspondent's reply than had been the case in the past.

There was a slight overlap in the post, so Matthew started his next letter before receiving Nigel's reply.

Dear Nigel
We have a new boy in the class. His name is Sean. He is a nicse boy. He has good manners. It was your turn to rite but it dos not matter. are you well? My han put my name on the ester egg are you haveing a hics ester. I have two eggs. We had an old techre in the teiter worct shop it was the old days. I did not hert miselif on my go kart gust a scrach I can go at 40 wich is the top speed. From

We have a new boy in the class. His name is Sean. He is a nice boy. He had good manners. It was your turn to write but it does not matter. Are you well? My nan put my name on an Easter egg. Are you having a nice Easter. We had an old teacher in the theatre workshop. I did not hurt myself on my go-cart. I can go at 40 [mph] which is the top speed.

Although this letter was not as long as the previous one, it was long by Matthew's standards. It showed his ability to handle a number of topics in coherent units. Each of the five topics was clearly grouped and for each topic there was some expansion, either in the form of additional information or in the form of a comment. The personal comment was a feature which occurred fairly regularly in Matthew's letters and the "but it does not matter" was a perfect example of his involvement in the subject matter on which he wrote, and his understanding of the rules of the exchange.

Matthew's letters were at last showing very clear progress. It had taken a long time for this spurt of growth to take place. It might be that a different kind of intervention could have resulted in the changes occurring earlier. However, we think that this late development demonstrates that children progress in different and uneven ways. Early intervention may not only have been confusing to him but may also have put him off developing as a vibrant and interesting writer. Despite his difficulties, Matthew has never avoided writing. Such an attitude is a very precious thing.

JAYNE

At the start of the exchange, Jayne had very little confidence as a writer. She was most reluctant to spell words for herself and, although she was aware of sound/symbol relationships, she found it difficult to analyse words. Being a resourceful child, she would search the classroom for items against which to check a word. Consequently, it took her some considerable time to write two or three lines, and it is against this background that the selection of the content and form of her early letters must be considered.

Her first letter was wholly a reference to the only shared experience between herself and Nigel.

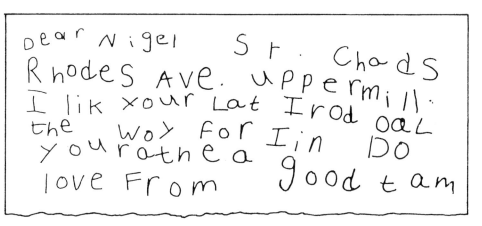

I like your letter. I read it all the way through. Did you have a good time?

This was a legitimate strategy but offered Nigel no new information. However, she did ask Nigel a question which demonstrated a commitment to the exchange. Nigel asked Jayne about her favourite toy.

Do you have a favourite toy? Do you have any teddy bears?
My wife still has a teddy bear that she was given when she was
a little girl.

*I did enjoy your letter. It was very nice. My favourite toy is a dog. It was
my mum's dog when she was a little girl. I live in Fernthorpe Avenue.
I can't see the hills from my house.*

Jayne's reluctance to generate her own topics created some
difficulties for her correspondent. It meant that Nigel was always
having to take the lead. He had to comment on her responses, ask
her related questions, and introduce new topics by asking more
questions. This pattern continued throughout the early stages of
the correspondence. Nigel in his reply to her second letter asked:
"Do you like reading? What are your favourite books?" She took up
the invitation.

Dear nigel F in Yoi D Yr Lit my
toy is covd Vicky my Dies
tib Book is
and the turnip B ie S MONSTER
are nas. love From the Books

MONSTER and the
magic umbrella

I enjoyed your letter. My toy is called Vicky. My best book is called Monster and the Turnip. The books are nice.

She again left Nigel looking for something to say which could carry the dialogue along. He chose to maintain the book theme.

One of my favourite books is Funny Bones. Do you know it. It is all about a group of skeletons that go around trying to frighten people. They certainly frightened me! Perhaps you can find the book in the school library? Do write and tell me what you think of it.

He also mentioned that Easter was coming up. Jayne again responded to Nigel's questions and for the first time seemed to assert herself with a significant question (see over).

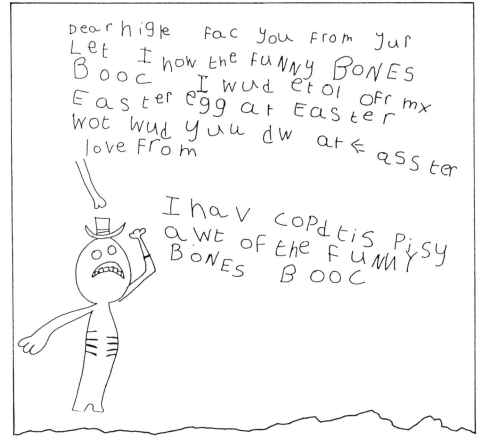

Thank you for your letter. I know the Funny Bones book. I would eat all my Easter eggs at Easter. What would you do at Easter? I have copied this picture out of the Funny Bones book.

She had asked a question in her first letter but in that context it had related back to a shared experience and had the function of cementing a relationship rather than extending the dialogue. Here she looked forward to a forthcoming event. Thus for the first time Nigel was able to respond clearly to an initiative of hers.

I went to a butterfly farm. I have never seen so many wonderful butterflies. They were very beautiful.

Nigel also sent a postcard of the butterflies.

I DOW like the butterflies I wet
Too cross keys I had a good time
thankyou foR yuR Let I lat yuR
postcard I got sam nuw clos

I do like the butterflies. I went to Cross Keys. I had a good time. Thank you for your letter. I like your postcard. I got some new clothes.

The pattern of these early exchanges was very clear. Jayne was always happy, indeed eager, to respond and was prepared to put considerable effort into responding; but by and large the content of her letters was predetermined by Nigel. She did not provide unsolicited information. Even so, her own voice came through, her opening remarks varied and were an expression of genuine pleasure. It is worth noting that Jayne was the only child who consistently used illustrations in her letters. However, she was using the drawings not to make her points, but simply to accompany them.

Later on in the exchange, Nigel received two letters at much the same time. In his reply, he chose first to pick up on the drawing that had accompanied the earlier letter.

Thank you so much for your letter, and thank you especially for the wonderful drawing of me in the spotlight. It did look a bit like me except that I have not got any red trousers. I used to have some red velvet trousers with white stars on, but that was a long time ago.

Nigel's reference to the trousers was picked up by Jayne, who obviously wrote with Nigel's letter in front of her *(see over)*.

Fhank ayou   For   your   letter   Do you
now   that   I   have   Some   Phpal
Sillck   ones   Ples   Can   you   Dror
me   a   Picher   if you   have
time   I have   a lot   of   Shells
have   you ?   I   have   a   Verey   lot
Of them   what S   your   Best   noßere
min   is 12   wat   is your   Best
Color   min   is   Pnuul   whot is
your   Best   whot   is   your   Best
hobey   I   have   lot I   can   not
Pich   I   have   lots   of letters
of yours   But   I   wooD   have
more   Bey   Cas   I   have   lostsd
a lot

Thank you for your letter. Do you know that I have some purple silk ones? Please can you draw me a picture if you have time? I have a lot of shells, have you? I have a very lot of them. What is your best number? Mine is 12. What is your best colour? Mine is purple. What is your best hobby? I have a lot. I cannot pick. I have a lot of letters of yours but I would have more because I have lost a lot.

Jayne's failure to contextualise her reply is fairly typical of her letters so far. The possibility that Nigel might not remember what he had written about trousers was not considered. Jayne asked a lot of questions in this letter. Perhaps she was, like Mark and Matthew, experimenting with questions. She did not ask questions to which she already knew the answers, as they did. She was no longer just responding to Nigel's letters. She now owned her part of the dialogue.

None of Jayne's questions were answered by Nigel who at this point sent a lengthy letter to the whole class. This was Jayne's reply.

> Than kyou for your letter.
> well not my letter. eveybodeys letter
> I was of. on monday I was sike.
> So I cud not lesen to mrs magson
> say it out bub a fuow more where
> of and they read it out to me
> it was pindedup on the wall like
> you wanted it So eveybody cud
> read it I am flying to jurser
> and I have got a swming pool
> out Side are Salaly I cannot
> wayt till I go on holiday I have
> no packd my bag yet you did
> do a big letter do you now how
> old I am Jayne is ____ do you now
> whot it is I hope they wont
> be cocris on the plan my bruver
> Said they will be he is. howays
> hating cocey how are you

Thank you for your letter. Well, not my letter. Everybody's letter. I was off. On Monday I was sick. So I could not listen to Mrs Magson say it out but a few more were off and they read it out to me. It was pinned up on the wall like you wanted it so everybody could read it. I am flying to Jersey and I have got a swimming pool outside. I cannot wait till I go on holiday. I have not packed my bag yet. You did do a big letter. Do you know how old I am? Jayne is ———. Do you know what it is?

It was this letter that crystallised the changes which had been taking place in Jayne's control of her letter writing. From failing to contextualise her information in previous letters, she here provided a very detailed set of explanations. She had gained confidence as a letter writer. She could now write at some length and was no longer dependent upon copying words.

Jayne was a close friend of Mark, and shortly after he included a story within a letter, so did Jayne. Her story was about a cat. Nigel's response mentioned bonfire night, Christmas and the cat.

Jayne skilfully used each of Nigel's topics in her reply.

I did not have a tarey Good time on Bonfire Night We did Not do eney thig But Me and Mark Went to my Nest door naber But I do Not Now them So much we wased the fire wecs Over the wall at Crhismas I am Mosley Ceting Clows But I am geting a Gaffeld tedey have I told you that I have had my Berthday I got a cat a rell one he is Calld Jethro he is so I will drow a piter of Jethro Some Cats Do not like water But wide Cat Do

I did not have a very good time on bonfire night. We did not do anything. But me and Mark went to my next door neighbour but I do not know them so much. We watched the fireworks over the wall. At Christmas I am mostly getting clothes but I am getting a Garfield teddy. Have I told you that I have had my birthday? I got a cat, a real one. He is called Jethro. He is 80. I will draw a picture of Jethro. Some cats do not like water but white cats do.

The bonfire was elaborated with details of the circumstances in which she watched the fireworks. She replied directly to a question about presents which allowed her to introduce Jethro the cat. This in turn led to a confused response to the question relating to her story in the previous letter. While this was not a particularly exciting letter, it nevertheless demonstrated clear control over the organisation of the text.

Although Nigel wrote first after Christmas, Jayne had already started to write a letter to him. This was completed before Nigel's letter arrived. Upon receiving Nigel's letter, Jayne then wrote a second letter, both of which were sent to Nigel at the same time. In the first one, completed before Nigel's reply had been received, she devoted the whole of the letter to one theme.

My Mum is going to go to Spain. So am I. and if my mum likes it she mhite live there. I do not want to. I have not bheh to Spain ever befor. I have bhen on a plan 4 times bake and forwadj bake and forwed s. and then I wold have bhen on a plain 6 times. I will draw a pithar of a Room whot I think my Room in Spain will look lilce. I am staying in a holetl. I have never bhen in one befor.

I do not want to go in a way. and I do in an way. I will drow a pithere whot I think my Room in Spin will look like.

Most of this letter constructed a scenario which led up to the delightful comments, "I do not want to go in a way. And I do in a way". It would be difficult not to sympathise with someone faced with wanting and yet not wanting to do something, especially when it involved moving into the unknown. It was relatively rare for any of the children to be as reflective as Jayne was in that letter. Did it reflect something of the considerable turmoil that such a change would cause in her life? It is almost as if she were using the letter to explore her feelings towards the event.

In the meantime, Nigel's letter arrived; it had picked up on the content of her earlier letter. In particular he commented on pets:

I did love the picture of Jethro. That is an unusual name. I wonder why it is called Jethro? I have never had a cat. I always felt that they needed a bit too much looking after. If you want to go on holiday you have to find someone to look after them. I think that I am too lazy to look after pets. Now that we do not have any snakes I do not think we will have any more pets.

> Thankyou for your letter. Rembar when you wroton to me when you put Jethro is a funny name we do not no if it was called that Cause we have got a fenid called Steve and he gave me the cat for my brithday Cause he has a dog So he fond Jethro a long time ago So he named him Jhethro

Remember when you wrote to me when you put Jethro is a funny name? We do not know if it was called that because we have got a friend Steve, and he gave me the cat for my birthday because he has a dog. He found Jethro a long time ago so he named him Jethro.

This is an example of a child wrestling with some rather awkward ideas. It was extremely rare for any child to aid their correspondent as clearly as Jayne did in her opening statement. For the most part, the children seemed to assume that Nigel or Les would remember what they had written. It may well have been Jayne's perception of the potential confusion of all the letters crossing over that led her to be so explicit. It served to open the topic but the difficulty of trying to sort out the relationships almost proved too much for her.

Nigel then replied to both letters and picked up mainly on the possible move to Spain. However, once again there was an overlap and Jayne started to write to Nigel before his reply had been received (*see over*).

We have a nuw Boy in are Class. His name is Sean. He Said He is my freind. I can not wat to the Easter. I hope you are doing Some thing nice. I am Oliey haveing my easter eggs. I am going to go to Spain FOR To weeks. I Can not wait. We went to Granda TV it was we went with the School. We went to Bradford musem it was good We went with the School we went to the Oldham wherck Shop that was good.

Friday 17th March.

I have Just got your letter thankyou for the letter if I do Move to Span I will go in a inlisch Shcool but I wlod haved to len Sponis Soon.

PS
Tankyou for your letter.

love

We have a new boy in our class. His name is Sean. He said he is my friend. I cannot wait to Easter. I hope you are doing something nice. I am only having my Easter eggs. I am going to Spain for two weeks. I cannot wait. We went to Granada TV. We went with the school.

76

We went to Bradford museum. It was good. We went to the Oldham workshop. That was good.
Friday 17th March.
I have just got your letter. Thank you for the letter. If I do move to Spain I will go in an English school. I would have to learn Spanish soon. PS Thank you for your letter.

In the absence of Nigel's reply, Jayne was again forced to generate her own topics. Even so, she managed to incorporate a relation-maintaining sentence into her letter. The rest of the letter was essentially a catalgoue of information. Once Nigel's reply arrived, she was able to go back to the Spanish theme in which there was still a sense of wistfulness in the way she writes.

In two years of letter writing, we have seen Jayne develop from a hesitant but persistent writer who seemed only to be able to respond to Nigel's lead, to a writer who is able to call on a range of strategies and has entered fully into a reciprocal relationship.

ELIZABETH

At the start of the exchange, Elizabeth was already a confident writer who wrote easily and quickly and used fairly conventional spelling. Her first letter, although short, showed that she clearly understood the need to provide information for her new correspondent. She listed the important people in her world.

Dear Nigel
I am 5 I am nealy 6
I have got a brother his name
is michael. I have got a mum
her name is Tina I have got
a dad to He live away from
me Love from

Elizabeth had set an agenda relating to families, and Nigel responded to and extended this theme.

Your birthday is soon and it is on the same day as my brother. I usually forget to send him a card. Do you think you will get lots of cards? Is your brother older or younger than you? My brother is younger than me.

Elizabeth maintained the theme but introduced new information for Nigel and had a go at contextualising her information by offering the date.

> Dear nigel
> My brother is alway hitting me I do not like my brother yesterday in the 11 of March He did not stop hitting me I had a dog and a Nanna but They died and I had other but That Nanna died Love

In that letter Elizabeth was able to expand the responses, which enabled her to take more of an equal role in the exchange. She did not pick up on Nigel's opening about her birthday, so Nigel tried again in his next letter. This time she responded.

> Dear Nigel I had a nice birthday and I Got Lots of presents my brother he dose not like me but now we have Got Some budgies Ther names are bill and Peter Peter makes a mes

In this third letter, Elizabeth still responded to what were by now well established themes. However, she was not simply a responder to Nigel's themes, as Jayne was. By offering new information in the way she did, Elizabeth negotiated the development of those themes.

Once the budgies were mentioned, Nigel was the one who did the following.

How nice to have some budgies. What colour are they? Why don't you draw me a picture of Peter and Bill? Do they never say anything or do they just go 'cheep cheep'?

78

It could be argued that Elizabeth was controlling some of Nigel's responses. What was of interest is that Elizabeth managed to do this for eight months without ever asking Nigel a question. This confidence as a writer was reflected strongly in her fourth letter which, unlike all the others, was sent from home.

friday 10th of APirL
to NigeL I know a baby
that keeps saying stand up.
to her mumum and once
I Gave her mummy.
a flower

an d she Kept Geting it. Of her
my God mother Got me Some
ear rings for my Birthday
and they lihte up when you
turn them on. and that
baby
once Keeps turning them on
she came to
house for tea and What
ever I had she had
from

In this letter from home, Elizabeth showed that she was able to maintain a theme across a whole letter. At first the earrings seem to be a sidetrack but prove not to be. Elizabeth pulls them into the theme, and it is clear that the whole letter represented a coherent text for her. It allowed Elizabeth to generate a much more complete message than before. The reader was offered information that rounded out the portrait of the baby, and left a much more complete picture than those of the budgies or her brother. Did being at home enable her to act more like an adult writer?

Nigel had to respond to the content of Elizabeth's letter, so again she had led the dialogue. His letter arrived after the school's Easter holiday, so he was able to offer information about his holiday and enquire about hers.

Dear Nigel I had a
a Good Holiday and I
went to oldham
sPoRts centre. to Go
Swimming with my Daddy.
and I had five easter
eggs and one of them
was wite chocklate
and it tasted like
a milky bar Love from

This letter showed that her previous experimentation with punctuation was not a one-off event. The letter was more typical of the first three than her fourth. For Elizabeth, there was clearly a distinction between what was appropriate at school and what was appropriate at home.

As the exchanges progressed, Elizabeth's control over her writing continued to grow. She also continued to write to Nigel from home as well as from school. One of these letters illustrated clearly how she was reaching for ways to express more subtle meanings in her writing.

Thankyou for your letter
but I lost it
did I say if you could come
to my party or did I ask
you if you could come to my
house on my Birthday
if I asked you on my
Birthday can you come
on friday the 18th march
or if it was My Party
it would be Sunday march 13th
if you coud come to my
Birthday if you went
you could come for tea.

Clearly Elizabeth was struggling here. However, it was precisely because she was trying to be more ambitious and cope with the rendering of meanings which have complex logical relationships that she found it so tough. The additional problem lay in trying to deal with different time sets within one sentence. The reference back was to a letter which itself referred forward with an invitation. At the same time, she was in the present but extending another invitation forward. Thus she was trying to handle the past, the present, and the future in two sentences. This pushed her into handling the 'if . . . then' construction. Although this was difficult for her, confidence in herself as a writer meant that she had a go.

This letter also offered an explanation of why she was writing from home *(see over)*.

do you Know why I
write to you at home
because I have normally
so mutch to tell you I
would prolably have to use
3 pages. I bet you Dont
Recognise my writeing did you
do you know Les's address
because I thoght it would
be good if I could write to
you at school and home
an write to Les Just at
Home.

The extent of Elizabeth's commitment to writing letters was clear. Like some of the other children, Elizabeth used a rhetorical question as a contextualising device in this middle group of letters. By this means, she could set up a new topic while at the same time dialogically drawing her reader along with her.

Nigel replied at some length to this letter.

Another lovely surprise; a long and quite enchanting letter from you. I'm sorry that you lost my letter. I did say in it that I wouldn't be able to come to your birthday party as I would be in London. So you'll have to make do with a birthday card. I hope you like it. I enjoyed choosing it for you. You say your party was last Sunday – so I've missed that. I bet you had a wonderful time. Did you get lots of presents?

Despite the number of topics here, the birthday theme got the major response.

> Thankyou for the birthday card
> you sent me I got alot of birthday cards and
> Guess what I got a tV set of my mum
> because we had 5 tv Sets So as there
> Was know Room In my Brother's Room know
> Room in my Room Know Room in my Mums Room
> and Know Room in the kichen and know
> Room in the living Room So as my Birthday
> Was coming up she gave it to me

In sustaining the theme, Elizabeth ran into some constructional problems, but again those problems were the consequence of her willingness to generate complex meanings.

Despite Nigel's general reply in which he raised a number of topics and responded to some of hers, Elizabeth created a new agenda in her next letter.

> Thankyou for your letter
> do you know what I went on a
> two hour trec in the Holidays
> it was For horse Riding
> and I vent all over
> Saddleworth in two hours But we
> went in every Short cut So that's
> why it was a two hour trec
> and when I came back we
> asked if I could go on an other
> trec and She Said yes So a
> week and a day later I went
> on the next trec

Elizabeth had written about horse riding before but her increasing age meant a greater freedom to spend more time out riding and to go on longer treks. The extent of this interest was more and more reflected in her letters. However, she was at the same time developing the ability to sustain her themes. So having more to say went alongside having more skill to say it.

These three letters from the middle of the exchange demonstrate Elizabeth's development as a letter writer. She continued to dominate the agendas but increasingly was using more complex language to express her meanings. Although she was not always successful, her willingness to take risks was a powerful indicator of her confidence as a writer.

Towards the end of the second year, Elizabeth was very secure in her letter writing. We have chosen to illustrate this by three dialogue exchanges with Nigel. It all began late one Autumn evening . . .

When I was riding
Misty back to the feild at Just after
nine we went wright next to Saddlew
orth church and I went with a fourteen
year old and a ten year old
We were Riding the Horses to the
feild and We Saw the Vicker
of the church leave and then we
herd a Scratching noise in the
Church and it defnetly not the
clock ticking and there was people at
the Side with torches I did enjoy
My Self but I wish I knew
what that scratching noise was.

Best Wishes

It is a simple and straightforward account but with an element of suspense in the last sentence. Nigel responded:

I loved your letter. It was all mysterious. You have got me wondering what that scratching noise was. Perhaps it was a ghost? Do you believe in ghosts? I don't. I've never seen anything even remotely like a ghost, so until I do I shall not believe in them.

Undaunted by Nigel's scepticism, Elizabeth made her position quite clear.

Thankyou for your letter
I believe in ghosts because once I saw
one and a lot of my friends have seen
them ─ ─ ─ ─
in Diggle there is a house and some
people say its haunted but it is big
enough to be haunted and old enough.

She did not simply make a claim but offered the testimony of others as evidence. She showed she understood some of the conditions for ghosts. Nigel replied:

So you have seen a ghost! What was it like? Where did you see it? What did it do? You must tell me all about it – it seems rather mysterious to see a ghost – were you frightened? I think I would be if a ghost suddenly appeared.

> Thankyou for your letter
> I cant discribe how the ghost looked
> like it was in the grave yard next to
> the church. it was Just walking
> around the graves Well you know
> When I told you about that
> Scratching noise in the church
> Well it was that night the Scratching
> noise probaly a ghost as well
> I was very frightend. No I
> was'nt drunk.

The ghost theme had been sustained over a period of eight weeks. Elizabeth's letters did include other topics and did explore more widely her horse riding experiences, but this exchange about the ghosts had a coherence and continuity which was relatively uncommon in any of the other children's letters.

We have not included Elizabeth's final letter of this two-year period, which was five pages long. At 402 words, it was the longest she had written to Nigel. Any letter which begins, "Now I have got some good news and bad news", is sure to hold the reader's attention, as well as indicating to the reader that some organisation lies behind the construction of the letter.

Elizabeth can use a range of letter-writing strategies which, although employed from the start, have become more refined as her experience has grown. She can effectively maintain a relationship with Nigel on her own terms, she can provide relevant and contextualised information, and she knows how to elicit responses from Nigel.

Conclusion

Each of the four children whose letters we have looked at in depth has developed quite distinctively. Each child's profile is unique. Although each received the same initial letter and replied from within the same classroom context, they went in their own directions. Whether they started as confident and capable authors or as authors who were still grappling with many problems, they all evolved – and in different ways. Such uniqueness characterises the letter writing of all the children in the class. It would have made no difference which children we chose. Their individuality makes it difficult to comment on the relationship between what the children featured in this chapter were doing and what all the other children were doing.

However, we feel that we can make six very general observations. The first is that all the children did develop as letter writers. Although some had long periods of apparent stagnation, changes of great significance eventually occurred. The second point is that the distinctness is a quality to be valued. Nothing would have been a greater distortion of the letters' validity than if they had arrived looking the same and saying essentially the same things in the same way. Instead, each child manifested his or her voice clearly.

The third observation is that the texts of the letters by the same child are uneven in quality. This is how it should be. It would be grossly unreasonable to expect any correspondent always to write with the same level of neatness, the same level of dynamism, at the same length, and with the same level of interest. The fourth point is that all the children were risk takers, although they did not all take the same level of risk. They were prepared to say what they meant rather than restrict themselves to only putting on paper what they could write.

The fifth point is that, throughout the two years and beyond, the children continued to be eager participants. The time and the effort never made the children want to stop the correspondence. It was clearly a very satisfying experience for them.

This may be related to our sixth point, which is that the children perceived themselves as partners in the exchange. Their correspondents had something to do with this, of course. The children were writing to someone who did not talk down to them, who freely exchanged ideas, and who did not chastise, complain, or criticise. Above all, they were corresponding with someone who wrote back to them as a partner. We feel that this comes across strongly in all the children's letters. They are clearly letters written by children, but they are not letters written to someone with superior status. They are letters written to someone who is a friend.

CHAPTER FIVE

Dedr Leg wer is Americer

THE LETTERS TO AND FROM AMERICA

The letters to Les deserve special consideration as they have the added dimension of dialogue between people from two similar but subtly different cultures. It was perhaps asking too much to expect five- to eight-year-olds to recognize these subtle differences. At the beginning of the correspondence, the children's geographical knowledge was understandably limited. They could hardly contemplate leaving home for a year and living in a country which was not their own, as Les had done. When he returned to the United States, they could not easily comprehend the distance nor the way his life might differ from their own. While in England, Les tried to minimise his American idioms and usage, while at the same time providing a wealth of information about his experiences as a visitor to England. Once back in the United States, he tried to give more information about his life there.

Les attempted to cross gaps in time and space by sending postcards of his area of the country to establish a frame of reference for the children. He first sent cards from the neighbouring Fargo, North Dakota/Moorhead, Minnesota area to show the cities, university and geography of his region. Whenever he travelled that year he sent cards: from Minneapolis, St Paul, Des Moines and Billings in America, and from New Zealand during his summer holiday.

All his letters and postcards were read with great interest, but to fully appreciate what was there the children would have had to objectify their knowledge of their own environment in order to make comparisons and connections. On the whole, they wrote to both Nigel and Les in the same way, exploring similar themes in similar ways. They reacted to the general human content of the letters rather than to their transatlantic origins. However, a few children began to show awareness of the special features, and to demonstrate understandings of the American relationship.

After one early exchange, some of the children searched a number of atlases and a globe to find North America, Minnesota and finally Moorhead. This activity was remembered 12 months later by two of the children who had been involved.

L *I was trying to find out where Minnesota was on the globe.*

R *I found it.*

L *Yes I have seen it, it's that way.*

R *That's north.*

L *It's at the top of North America but to one side – in the middle somewhere.*

This conversation is reflected in the correspondence between Les and one child. The child asked: "Where do you live?" Les responded by reporting: "I live in Stockport this year but I am from America. My usual home is in Minnesota. Do you know where that is?"

The child then asked: "Where in Minnesota. We looked for it in the book. We found it."

When Les replied with a clear description of where he lived, the reaction in the next letter was:

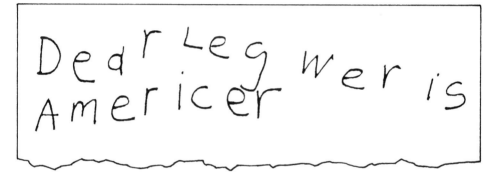

You can't win them all!

One of the youngest children in the class began by asking simple questions relating to Les's circumstances as a visitor to England. He could not easily understand that Les had a home in America and also rented one in England. He expressed surprise that an American should be without a car and struggled to find the words to convey this in his second letter (see over).

I NO YO UHaVnoyOUHaV Car
BeecoS peōp Rddot HavCar SI det PepoK HaV
C ars has has Cars I bet yoUHaV

I know you have a car because people do have cars. I bet people have cars.
I bet you have.

When Les returned to his home, the boy once more questioned him about his car. This concept of American cars will have been derived from TV and it is not surprising that his image is somewhat fanciful.

qbet yo4 hav poSh carA bet at berb iＱet in f qnSY wIyS oh the car worcuL rfs the Car the at yoUbraL

I bet you have a posh car. I bet it has a jet engine and fancy wheels on the car. What colour is the car that you've bought?

Les was able to report back:

I bought a new car this week. It is an Oldsmobile Tornado. I am very pleased with it. I feel like Night Rider in it.

After a display of road signs and symbols was mounted in the classroom, another child pondered about the difference between road signs in England and America. First he told Les that he had been collecting road works (meaning road signs).

Then, when Les asked him whether the signs were the same as in America, he spent a great deal of time and effort drawing some of the signs for Les, concentrating on the work for a much longer period than he usually did.

The road signs aren't the same in our country. I have drawn some for you.

When Les returned to America, the same child started to enquire about his life there *(see over)*.

Wot baw you byw at a meric baw yow gow shopig wer is Nigcl is he wiv you dou hav a garden is ycr hoysc dow yow hav a car drew you hav sum flcwers dew you hav hasiatal

What do you do at America? Do you go shopping? Where is Nigel? Is he with you? Do you have a garden in your house? Do you have a car? Do you have some flowers? Do you have a hospital?

The detailed reply Les sent was carefully read, especially the section describing the kind of work Les did. The boy continued to ask specific questions: "And my Dad goes to work. How many days do you work? You get 3 pounds if you work all day I bet?"

Another child reflecting on Christmas in England asked about American customs: "We are at school now. Do you put decorations up?"

One boy had received a postcard which featured a picture of the Minnesotan State bird, the loon. The postcard generated a number of questions: "Do you walk around the lakes in Minnesota? Do loons fly? Are the lakes big?"

Another child, on receiving a similar card, wrote: "I think the loon looks sad. We have not got any in England. We have ducks and geese."

A selection of another girl's letters are of particular interest because she speculates about street lighting, reflects on the difference in the weather, and mentions her father's travels which she realises will interest Les particularly:

It has been hailstoning here.

Has it been doing it there?

Les responded, fully as usual:

As a matter of fact, last weekend we had sleet that melted and then it got real cold and froze. Later it snowed. People who had no garages for their cars had a hard time opening their cars and getting all the ice off.

Her question about the weather reflected a naive understanding of the distance which separated Les and herself, as it was unlikely that the weather in North America and England would be the same. When Les replied, he was able to give an example of the difference in extremity between his own experience and hers due to a recent storm.

The girl followed up this response in her next two letters:

When its night time does it light up? Because they have lamp posts in England and it lights up in the streets.

Dear Les My Daddy went to America and he went two days in American and two days in Boston, and two days in New York . . . I bet in Uppermill it snows and then its dry again in the morning . . . I hope that you house blow down.

Her question about lampposts highlights the limited understanding she has about life in America but also shows a realisation that there may be differences. She did, however, recognise that there was some bond with Les when her father visited the United States. For her, America, Boston and New York may be three different countries. The final reference is to her own life in Uppermill, where the snow does not stay long. Unfortunately, her last sentence does not say what she means because she left out the word 'doesn't'.

Les tried to answer the questions about the lampposts and the weather. Here again he emphasises the severity of winter in Minnesota, but she would still have difficulty visualising it – as would most adults in England since they are unlikely to have experienced temperatures as severe as Minnesota's.

Thanks for your last two letters. They both came on the same day so I will answer them together. How was your Daddy's trip to America? You must tell him if he ever gets close to me, he must ring me up.

Where I live there are lots of lampposts along the street and some are high, lighting the roadway. Some lower, lighting the yards. There are even some about three feet tall that light our walkways. Of course, when there is a blizzard you can't see anything . . . Never worry about my house in a blizzard. I only get worried during tornados.

The response to Les's suggestion about phoning him was revealing. All she provided was the name of the company her father worked for. There was no real understanding of why the phone call had been suggested. For her, Les's offer needed a reciprocal offer, and so she told him where her father worked. The lampposts were mentioned again:

My daddy's trip was lovely. If you ever want to phone my daddy up it is Mossley Special Belts Transmission. How many lampposts are there? If you can count the lampposts . . . I think my daddy liked New York best.

As always, Les took the idea seriously.

Thanks for the information about your daddy's business. I'll phone him there if I need to do so. I'm sorry I don't know the number of lampposts along the walks. They are small, only about a yard tall. I'll try to remember to count them when I get home.

Also relating to the weather was an interesting episode which occurred when Les wrote to a number of children about winter sports. Just about this time, the staff in school had warned the children about the dangers of fatal accidents on frozen ponds or canals.

Les had written:

The ground is all white with beautiful fresh snow. It feels like Christmas to me. I hope Father Christmas was good to you and that you had a lovely holiday. My daughter Meg is coming after Christmas and we will go to a resort. I love to ride snowmobiles on the frozen lakes. We race and go very fast.

The children were quick to pass on their concerns about such foolhardy activities.

You shouldn't go on the frozen ice because it can crack.

Please be careful in case you fall in.

Les reassured them: "You needn't worry. I won't fall in the lake. I won't go on until there is over 12 inches of ice."

And they were able to record their satisfaction: "I am glad that you don't go on the ice unless it is very deep."

Two children had a special link with America. One girl had lived there for a while, although she had been too young to remember much about it. This was the subject of a number of exchanges between her and Les and helped to establish a relationship between them.

> my sister is American because she was born in New york. I used to Live on Long Island. have you been to New york city. I want to go back to New york.

Although she didn't remember anything herself, the knowledge she gained from her parents is shown in the way she can separate New York State from New York City.

Les eagerly took up this theme:

> **The news in your letter really surprised me. I didn't know you had lived in New York or that your sister was born there. Yes, I have been to New York State and New York City a long time ago, but not for many years . . . You must write and tell me how you came to be in America.**

> I was born in england and then I went to America then Katie was born I went home and Emily was born I went to America. I do not know why I went to America. I now think it was because my Dad had a Job there.

In the above exchange she sequenced events with reference to the birth of her sisters and provided a concise explanation in answer to Les's question. Much later in the correspondence, she referred to America again. This was unprompted by Les and it was possible that she had only recently rediscovered her souvenirs.

I have been to Minneapolis when I lived in America and I have got a T-shirt from there.

Les asked for more details of the T-shirt.

My T-shirts are called Minnihaha Falls and Minneapple.

In a later letter she added:

I have given one of my T-shirts to Katie but I have found more American shirts.

For no obvious reason she reflected on America once again in a later letter, reminding Les about her sister and using an interesting strategy to link friends at home and abroad in her letter.

> One day I might come back to america to see my frends and remember Katie who was born in America (my sister). Soon I am going to go to my frends house who lives somewhere else and I am looking fowd to that. My frends in america are Andrew and Kate and lots more.

Another girl grew aware of her American contact when a holiday was planned. She normally wrote to Nigel, but when she knew she would be visiting America, she wrote to Les from home on her own initiative:

> Dear Les
>
> I wanted to write and tell you that I am going to America on october 14th I am going with my mummy Daddy sister and nan we will be staying in orlando and we are going to see Disneyworld and Sea world. Do you live near orlando and have you been to Disneyworld

A dialogue then developed about her forthcoming trip, as well as other joint interests. The following excerpts from her letters illustrate this well:

I will tell my Mum that we won't see you when we go to America. I am very excited and I can't wait till I go. I hope it is fun.

I am going to America because my sister went when she was eight. Now she is sixteen. Since she has been to America my mum promised that I could go and that is why I am going to America.

Did she have a good time in America? Les didn't find out because of the intervening time factor, but Nigel heard in his letter from her after the trip *(see over)*.

It was very nice in America we went to wet and wild, in the morning and other mornings we stayed by the pod. and at night we went to a show called Madi grah. a wild west night called fort liberty, and other nights we went to lestarents, somtimes we went to crazy golf. and then a restront. We went to Disney World and I went to mickeys birthday party and I also went on the fasted rolla costa in the world. I liked it a very lot.

She makes it sound great, doesn't she?

Finally, it appears that even the youngest of Englishmen see the need to explain to an American that most English of institutions – the game of cricket.

IS a bit like In summer I play crikit. crikit base ball. but you run when you have hit the ball a long way and the wikit keeper can get you out when the Boller has bolld G bollwilB another one comes

In summer I play cricket. Cricket is a bit like baseball but you run when you have hit the ball a long way and the wicket-keeper can get you out. When the bowler has bowled six balls, another one comes.

There, doesn't that explain everything!

On the whole, only a little use was made of the American connection. The letters indicated that, not surprisingly, for the most part these young children seemed to view Les as a person rather than as an example of a different kind of culture. But we feel that for some children, the experience of having to face up to cultural differences in letters did encourage them to reflect upon their own lives. Thus some of them, and perhaps others in a more vicarious sense, did have their cultural and geographical horizons expanded as a result of the letters to and from America.

CHAPTER SIX

I Thinck   my   Sist has riT To you?

SHARING AND EXTENDING

The letters that Nigel and Les wrote were to a restricted group of children. However, as the exchange of letters continued, it had an influence upon other children in the school. We want to report on this as an indication that a letter-writing project may have more benefits to offer to a school than may be apparent at first.

Although the letters to the children in Anne's class were intended as private correspondence, the notion of privacy did not last long. After just a few weeks, it was obvious that the children were sharing their letters with each other. In the first instance, it was probably between friends who sat close to each other. Anne had noticed that the children would pause in their reading and point out interesting sections to the child nearby. Before long, casual conversations in the class revealed a great deal of shared information. Evidence of knowledge about other people's letters can certainly be seen in some of the children's responses to Nigel and Les.

At that point Anne decided to use that common knowledge as a basis for a whole-class activity. Each child was asked to add something that they knew about either Nigel or Les to a list. The result was an interesting exercise in analysing information. For example, while many children knew that Nigel had some pet snakes, fewer children could name them, and only one child knew what type of snakes they were. Deductive inference was also required. They knew that Nigel had a brother called Clive. They also knew that Nigel had a niece called Emma. Was it possible that Clive was Emma's father? A similar problem was posed by information from Les. They deduced that Les had been the baby of his family.

The information about Nigel and Les was collated, illustrated and made into a big book for everyone to share. In fact, the class then shared it with the whole school at the beginning of a book week. This was the first inkling for many of the other children that something special was going on in Anne's class.

When Nigel and Les made a return visit with one of Nigel's snakes, the news that Infant Two had a very special visitor was conveyed by word of mouth in the playground. Everybody knew there was a snake in school (although whether everybody was secure about it was another matter). Thus, even when Anne left the school, most of the children in other classes knew that a letter exchange was going on.

The first real extension of the letter writing took place early in the next year of school. Because of staffing problems, Anne's class was split up and mixed in with two other classes. When Nigel's letters arrived for the children who had been in Anne's class, they were shared with new classmates. The other children recognised something interesting and all wanted to write as well. As new children arrived in the school on occasion and were assigned to that class, they joined the group of correspondents. Nigel and Les found the number of letters to them was growing.

I am writing to say that I have never written to you before.

I am a new girl and all my friends are writing to you so I am.

I am a new boy here. I hope you are having a nice time wherever you are.

What could Nigel and Les do but reply?

Many of these letters will one day repay further investigation into how children cope with writing to someone totally unknown to them and who they probably never expect to meet.

For Les, the sharing and new contacts arose in a different way. On his return to Minnesota, he sent a collection of postcards to help the children gain some insight into his life back home. These were shown to the whole school. One of Les's cards in particular created such interest that many children, including those from other classes, used it as a stimulus for writing stories.

Les expressed his surprise in a letter to Anne and Nigel:

I never knew that anyone would get a story from them. I was just charmed by the stories about the Ice Palace from the older children, and they provided an interesting contrast with those from the younger children.

The headteacher explained to us what had happened.

We have a message board in the hall and those sorts of things are put on it so that all the school can see. And then again when special letters came, we began to make more of it. We began to make a point of telling everybody in the school that letters had come from Nigel and Les and eventually some of the whole class letters and cards were shared with the whole school.

The sending of the stories to Les created a contact for which some of the other children may have been waiting: a chance to join in. They really wanted to be involved. The headteacher told us:

A child came one day and said, "I've got a letter for Les." She was not one of the sample. And then some more of her friends (who had brothers and sisters already writing) picked up on what was happening.

One of the original writers had told Les about his sister's interest. He wrote:

My sister has written to you or is going to.

Extracts from the older children's letters showed how they introduced themselves:

My sister writes to Nigel. She writes to him a lot and he writes back. She has got a lot of things off him like letters, postcards, and Christmas cards. She keeps them in a brown envelope. When she has gone I have a look at all her things. It's fun to have a look.

My brother writes to you. He pins his letters from you on his notice board. I am nine years old. I also have a brother called . . . who is four.

I have a friend called . . . She writes to you. It's easy for her because she has got a brother who writes to you. I don't know what to write.

By November 1981 the original letter-writing project had expanded widely. "It snowballed, really, didn't it!" said the headteacher.

Letter writing has now become a feature of life in the whole school. According to the headteacher:

It has had other spin-offs too. Practically every child in every class in the school now writes to somebody. The older children write to sailors on board ship (through a family connection), and some write to an American teacher who spent some time teaching in our school while on an exchange visit. Others write to children in another school.

When the three of us visited the school two years after the exchange had begun, there was a substantial display outside the classroom of the sections of letters that Nigel had written while on his round-the-world trip. They were accompanied by the photographs he had sent. Thus something which had been written for one group of children became available for all the children.

This raises one important issue. If this happens, does it alter the interaction between the two writers who may no longer see their letters as something essentially private? On the whole we feel it did not. As long as each child received their letter privately, the personal nature of the exchange seemed to be preserved. The subsequent sharing did not detract from the fact that the letter was originally sent to a particular child. It is important to realise that in the case of this school, the public sharing arose out of the children's decision to share their letters with each other, with teachers, brothers and sisters, and with parents. It was not an illogical step to make appropriate letters available to a wider audience within the school.

From the school's point of view, the project had stimulated a great deal of interest in writing. It was no longer seen as an academic exercise. It had become a purposeful and highly meaningful activity for all the children.

CHAPTER SEVEN

I Do still like writing letters and I am going to write lots more

THE CHILDREN REFLECT ON LETTER WRITING

Throughout our project and in this book, we have been acting as spectators, mostly on the children's texts, but also to a lesser degree on Les and Nigel's. Alongside this spectating has been quite a lot of interpretation of the children's interests, attitudes, feelings, thoughts, and abilities. We would only be telling a part of the story if we failed to allow the children to be their own spectators. In this chapter, the children themselves reflect and comment on letter writing. The first section deals with comments made by the children in their letters. The second and third sections look at the oral comments made by the children in interviews, when they reflected upon their letter writing.

IN THE LETTERS

On the whole, there are very few comments about writing letters in the letters. This should not surprise us. The purpose of writing letters is not to act as commentators on the writing process, but to exchange information and ideas. Language has a transparency in that, providing the experience is purposeful, we tend to use it without being aware of the ways in which we produce it. This applies as much to writing as it does to speaking.

The comments in the letters fall into the three broad categories: 'letter writing as pleasure', 'letter writing as a way of knowing people' and 'letter writing as a process'.

Letter writing as pleasure
There were quite a few short statements expressing pleasure in writing letters:

Writing is my hobby. It is very easy.

I do still like writing letters and I am going to write lots more.

I love getting letters too.

I like writing letters too.

It is our belief that these statements truly reflect the enjoyment that the children have had from being taken seriously as correspondents. When so much writing that is done in schools is not seen by children as pleasure, it gives us great satisfaction that our correspondents have had so much fun. We know that it has been hard work for some of them much of the time, and for all of them some of the time – as indeed it has been for us – but they have persevered not out of duty, but because they wished to.

Letter writing as a way of knowing people

In chapter 2 we said that many of the children's first letters reflected a view that such correspondence was either 'I'll tell you all about me' or 'I want to know more about you'. For the most part, this was evident by the children actually offering information or requesting it. It was rare for a child to say outright that letter writing is a way of knowing people. However, it happened on a few occasions.

> I Like writing to you very much please will you write to me again Because I will write to you again and when I do I will Tell you lot's of Thing's

This letter, part emotional request, part offer, demonstrates explicitly the relationship between letter writing and knowing people. So does this extract: "Do you know all about me and will you write and would you write to me?"

The next letter combines statements of pleasure with a view of what it is that is so satisfying about letter writing – knowing people! (See next page.)

THANK you FOR all THe
letters you HAve Ritten TO me
I will keeP on Ritti9 TO you
and. I HoPe you will keeP
on RiTTin9 ro me and I
like RiTTin019 leTTeRS To You
I Like RiTTin9 Toyou Because
youcAn dRAW PictuRes and
find out THings.

It was a wonderful letter for Nigel to receive.

Letter writing as a process
If we were strictly accurate, there would be no examples in this section but we have identified a few extracts that seem to be close.

I bet it takes you a very long time to write all those twenty-one letters. It takes me about half an hour to write one and my hand hurts as well.

I like the writing processor and it is neat and I don't mind if you do make a mistake.

Do you know why I write to you at home? Because I have normally so much to tell you I would probably have to use three pages.

We were also able to identify three statements that, although not explicit about the mental processes involved in writing letters, seem to represent knowledge about letter writing processes. What makes them so interesting is that such thoughts have been written so overtly:

I know that you've heard about Emma has left. Its just that I like mentioning it.

Now that's enough about football.

Yum all that talking about eggs has made me hungry.

In each of these statements, the child has ceased being the straightforward writer of a message and has stepped into a different role: that of commentator. Such occasions were rare indeed in the letters.

Interviews after one year

Anne maintained contact with the children even though she had left the school. Almost one year after the exchange had begun, she returned to school to talk with the children about their experience. Although by now we were beginning to realise that the dialogue would continue indefinitely and that we wished to use the data in a more formal way, the interview was seen as informal. The idea of a highly structured set of questions presented in a formal setting would have been in conflict with the nature of the whole exchange.

Small groups of children came to talk to Anne in a quiet area and chatted generally about the letter writing experience. With all the groups, mention of Nigel and Les produced smiles and other indications of excitement and pleasure. After referring back to the first visit, the children were asked how they now felt about writing and receiving letters.

There was general consensus that they enjoyed it. Some children found it difficult to express these feelings other than saying it made them feel "happy" or that it "excited" them. One child expressed this in concrete terms: "I like writing because you can find out about people and ask them questions."

When another child was asked if she still felt excited even though she knew who the letters were from, she said: "I know, but I like getting letters."

Others implied their continuing pleasure in more obscure ways:

And I'm going to ask for his address so I can write to him at home.

Once I wrote and he put a picture at the bottom.

Or even more romantically:

I put a bow on the front and his name round it.

One child's response needed explaining.

M *'When I open them there's always scrap paper on the floor.*

A *How do you mean?*

M *Well, I always throw it on the floor.*

Then Anne remembered that when the letters arrived, the classroom had always looked as if the waste basket had been emptied on the floor. In their eagerness to get to the letters, the children discarded the envelopes hastily. What better way to say "I can't wait".

At one point in the exchanges, one of the children had sent Nigel and Les an Easter egg each. This incident was remembered and the child who sent it recalled receiving a book as a thank you present. She also remembered clearly Les's special story for her about his childhood. This led to recalling other book gifts from Les with appreciation. Other things were also remembered, like Les saying "I want to talk English like you". The children concluded that he had an American accent and only some of his words were not like theirs. The search for Minnesota on the globe was remembered vividly and this sparked off another significant memory:

He sent a Christmas card about sledging on the lakes but Mrs Shearing said we were not to slide on the lakes!

The discussion demonstrated the rather confused concept the children had about America when one child said, "The Waltons know Les because he lives near them." There was general consensus that, because the family of the TV programme lived in the United States, Les was likely to know them. The touch of fantasy was taken further when a child remembered his letter writing experience before Nigel and Les had come to school:

T *I remember what kind of letters we used to write before. We wrote to Fairy Tales.*

A *Yes, so we did.*

T *And that person got the wrong wolf!*

More than 12 months after the event, the truth was coming out. When Anne had replied to a letter as the 'Wolf' she wrote as the wrong wolf!

T *I was meaning the wolf in the* Seven Little Kids *and it came from the wolf in the* Three Little Pigs.

The children began to discuss who had written the earlier replies. Several said "It was you" to Anne, but even a year later they were hedging their bets: "Well, it might have come back from Walt Disneyland".

Interviews after two years
With Les returning to England for Christmas, 1988, we contacted the headteacher to make arrangements for us to visit the school. After almost two years, we were more certain about which of the issues we were most interested in. Nevertheless we did not conduct the interviews in a formal way. They were essentially a discussion between a child and one of us as the letters were perused. We raised our topics in the course of general, easy conversation.

Even after almost two years of corresponding, the children all agreed that they still enjoyed getting the letters. While most simply said that they felt pleased or excited when the letters arrived, some explained further that it was because they liked hearing about other people and what they had been doing.One child even said that she felt "proud to get letters", implying that it was a special privilege. To some extent, this may be because these are the only letters that most of the children will ever specifically receive as individuals while so young. The receipt of the letters may have helped them feel more grown up.

The importance to the children of the dialogue was also reflected in the high proportion of those who had kept all the letters. This reflected parental interest or support to some degree, and also the degree of control the children had over their own belongings. When we discussed what the children did with their letters and where they were kept, we got such answers as:

In a book like a photograph album.

In my desk.

On my notice board.

In a big folder.

One child explained how she had to keep them away from her dog who would attack any scrap paper left lying about, and another child appeared to have an over-tidy mum who was a constant threat to the preservation of the letters.

Further evidence of the pleasure derived from the letters was shown in the degree to which they were shared with other people. The majority of the children shared them with friends in school and, on occasions, with their parents.

Perhaps the most surprising thing about this second interview was the reaction of the children to seeing their early letters. This was the first time that they had seen all the letters together and we thought they would find them interesting. We did not anticipate that many might find them a bit disturbing. Some children looked at them uncomfortably while some expressed their shock quite explicitly:

They are horrible.

Those at the beginning are all scruffy.

I'm not very good now but I'm better than that.

As we talked more about this, we realised that they were to some extent embarrassed by their early attempts. Subsequently, we realised that the experience of looking back at early efforts was something from which most children were cushioned by the fact that such efforts are usually lost or left when the children go on to new classes.

Anne was able to put this in some perspective when she again listened to the tape of her discussions with the children after one year of the exchange. At one time in that discussion, the children focused on their earliest recall of writing:

J *When I was four I wrote a letter to my auntie.*

A *Did you do that yourself or did you copy it?*

J *I wrote it myself and when I was three I could even write like I can now but I was not very good at pictures so I just did a scribble at the end for my picture.*

A *So could you write before you could draw pictures?*

J *Yes.*

A *Well, I am surprised.*

J *Well I started off with scribble.*

A *Oh, I see; when you started off it was just scribbly lines.*

B *I could write when I was 2½.*

C *I could write well when I was two but I always got the spelling wrong.*

A *When did you start to write well.*

E *About three or four.*

The children remembered themselves as moving from scribble to acceptable writing at a relatively early age. There was almost an element of competition to see who could give the lowest age for when they could write. They all quite clearly were under the impression that by four or five years of age, when they started school, they could write quite well. Anne knew only too well how inaccurate that impression was!

Looking at their reactions when faced with their letters from two years previously, it is perhaps understandable that they were shocked. Here was proof that they had not been as good as they thought, even at five or six years old. They had no idea what level of performance is acceptable for very young children. They assumed that they had always been able to do what they could do now. It is little wonder that they reacted in the way they did.

Neither is it surprising that, when asked what they thought they had learned from the letter writing exchange, most of them focused on the surface features of their writing:

My letters are tidier now.

The writing is smaller.

I've learned to leave finger spaces.

Some children commented on their spelling:

I haven't missed out any letters.

I think about the sounds now and well, sometimes it's like 'startid', 'started', it's not the same.

There was a general feeling that the early letters had not been long enough and that length was a measure of progress:

The first letters needed to be longer.

My letters have got bigger.

When we directed the question more specifically to what they learned about writing letters, the children found it difficult to respond. Two children suggested that they knew more about meeting the needs of the audience:

I know how long it should be.

Not too much, not too long, he might get bored reading it.

More often, however, they interpreted the question to mean 'what had they learned about Nigel and Les'. Clearly our original question was too demanding for the children but they revealed in another part of the discussion that they did have some clear ideas about the requirements of letter writing. When we discussed how they selected what to write about, many children revealed that they had some self-imposed rules. They also saw themselves as writing balanced letters in which they responded to enquiries, in which they told their news, and in which they asked questions.

I answer the questions.

You have to answer all the questions.

Well, I answer all the questions and then tell him something and then ask some questions.

I read the letter and answer all the questions he has written to me.

I think about what I have been doing.

I tell the most important things.

Whether or not the children actually follow these 'rules' when writing the letters, it is nevertheless clear that they have a well developed set of strategies for thinking about letter writing. One child even justified the opening convention of 'thank you for your letter' by saying it was used "because he has taken the time to write to me".

Sometimes writing does not come easily. As one child explained:

Well, I'm writing this letter now and I can't think what to say. I've done all this work and I can't think what to say. It's in my tray and I'll just have to wait until I can think.

When asked if she ever did not want to write, another child said: "Sometimes I'm fed up or I'm tired but I still write back". Nigel and Les know that feeling only too well!

Even further proof that the exchange of letters has been successful was the response of the children when asked if they wanted to continue writing. The answer was an emphatic "yes".

The final issue discussed was whether the children would mind if we published some of their letters in a book to share with other teachers. From our point of view, a great deal depended upon their replies. Some answered unhesitatingly that they did not mind. Others were concerned that the early letters were not good enough to show. When we explained that we could change or hide the names so that only they would know which letters were theirs, they agreed that we could use them. Without that permission, this book could not and would not have been written.

CHAPTER EIGHT

So me day You will No all about me.

WHAT DOES IT ALL MEAN?

We hope that the reader of this book has enjoyed the story so far. It will have been clear that a good time was had by all, and that letter writing was an interesting and enjoyable event for the children and the adults. But is that it? Is it all simply saying the obvious? Was Mark correct? Do we now 'no' all about him? Or is there some significance in what has been going on that extends beyond 'having a good time'? Does knowing all about the children mean something more than being able to compile a list of their hobbies, friends, and interests?

In one sense, whether or not something is obvious depends on what one already knows. Anyone who is even vaguely familiar with recent work on young children's writing will not have been surprised at their enthusiastic response to the challenge of engaging in sustained letter writing with relatively unknown adults. But why has something which many would claim was obvious been the subject of so little critical scrutiny? A search of the major educational data bases would reveal that the letter writing of very young children has been almost totally neglected. Indeed, it is virtually only because of a relatively recent surge of interest in dialogue journals that anything relating to written dialogue and young children exists. We do stress 'young children'. Studies are more prevalent of children who are eight or nine years old.

We suspect that there are two factors influencing this apparent neglect. The first is that engaging in sustained correspondence with another person implies a commitment to a 'not present' audience. Are young children able to step outside their own perspectives and consider the needs of a distanced 'other'?

The second and related factor is the claim that children's earliest encounters with constructing written language are, inevitably, with story. Are they able to cope seriously with written language that makes different kinds of demands? Can they handle the techniques of written dialogue? Does the lack of study into young children's letter writing reflect a belief that the answer to these questions is no? After all, why investigate something which can have no payoff? At the heart of that doubt lies the intellectual demands that are made upon a writer when constructing a text for a distanced reader. Are those demands too great for very young children? Conventional wisdom has always said yes.

The notion of audience is central to this problem. As Rosen (1971, p. 142) said:

The writer is a lonely figure cut off from the stimulus and corrective of listeners. He must be a predictor of reactions and act on his predictions. He writes with one hand behind his back, being robbed of gesture. He is robbed too of his tone of voice and the aid of clues the environment provides. He is condemned to monologue; there is no-one to help ɔut, to fill the silences, put words in his mouth, to make encouraging noises.

In other words, to construct a text the writer has to learn to play both the parts of writer and reader extremely well. This view of writing represents what Newkirk (1985) has termed the 'heroic ideal of composing'. Certainly, if that is how it is done, then such an attempt is an ordeal for any writer but especially very young children. As put by Collins and Michaels (1986, p. 207):

The task is often difficult for any writer but it is especially so for children since it requires of the writer the special effort of distancing oneself from the present context into a non-existent yet imagined time and place. Such a transition of self in time and space requires the writer to make the inferential leap between placing the words on the page and their ultimate reception thereafter at some unspecified time and place.

The extent to which young children are aware of other people's perspectives is a topic that has been extensively debated. If audience awareness means anything, it must be the ability to understand to some degree the perspective of the other person. From a strictly Piagetian perspective, young children appear to have a somewhat egocentric stance towards others. However, it has become apparent (Donaldson 1978) that, as the context shifts to one which is more familiar, then young children's ability to decentrate increases. Put another way, as the authenticity of the experience grows, so does the child's ability to take more of the circumstances into account. The issue of 'authenticity' is an important one. Assumptions made by some researchers about children's writing seem to be based not on what children can do but on what they will do in certain contexts.

Most researchers studying young children's audience awareness have chosen to investigate them from age nine upwards. This may be because they agree with Hunt (in Nigrosh, 1985) that young child are not interested in writing. When Hunt studied grammatical structures in young children's writing, he started with fourth graders in the United States school system, explaining:

The fourth grade seemed a good place to begin. Before the fourth grade, children may jabber away with ease, fluency, and exuberance, but most third graders write only under considerable duress. (cit in Nigrosh p. 150)

Anyone reading the efforts of the children in this book must wonder what had been done to Hunt's fourth graders to make them such reluctant writers. Indeed, according to Graves (1983, p. 3): "Children want to write. They want to write the first day they attend school."'

A more probable reason why researchers have not looked at the audience awareness of young children is that they simply did not believe it would be there. They also seem to have chosen to explore audience awareness by means of highly inauthentic 'audience-adaptation' contexts. These are usually of the 'imagine you are writing to the Mayor to complain about . . .' sort which are then contrasted with a similar task related to a different audience (for an example see Nigrosh, 1985). It is interesting that, when Kroll (1984, p. 425) used more realistic tasks to examine the audience-adaptation of nine-year-olds, he was able to write.

> We must consider why the subjects in this study appeared to be so competent when in a number of other studies young writers have been portrayed as lacking in audience-adaptation skills. A likely explanation is that the communication task used in this study provided children both with an appealing occasion for writing, and with a plausible context for composing more than one message on the same topic.

Such letter writing was, of course, a one-off activity. We know of only two studies which have examined very young children's letter writing as extended interpersonal dialogue, Vargus (1983) and Rowcroft (1989), although J. Greene (1985), studied slightly older children. In both cases, the dialogue was pursued for only a short period of time. There are now many studies of dialogue journal communication – including some carried out with very young children (see Braig 1986, Hall and Duffy 1987, and Duffy 1989) – but letter writing poses problems that dialogue journals usually manage to avoid. These problems are mostly to do with the time that elapses between communications, and the fact that all the previous exchanges in a dialogue journal are available for inspection. In most studies involving dialogue journals of very young children, the exchanges have been very frequent and usually between the teacher and the children, or between the children and an adult working in the classroom.

The exchanges reported in this book clearly cannot answer questions relating to the audience-adaptation of very young children. We did not set the children the task of writing to different audiences. However, we do believe that the responses of the children make a contribution to the debate about young children's perception of audience. In chapter 2 we reported on the first letters written by the children. At that time, Les and Nigel were almost totally unknown to them. We found that the children used strategies which were wholly appropriate for writing a first letter to a stranger with whom one expects to build a relationship through written dialogue.

Were their strategies any different from those which would be used by more mature writers? Our many discussions about this with adults suggest not. Harste, Woodward and Burke (1984, p. 105) said about their study of very young children: "We have no evidence that children's psycholinguistic and sociolinguistic strategies are qualitatively different from the kinds of decisions which more experienced language users make."

We would want to add that it seemed to us as if the children were able to employ in their writing the interpersonal skills that they had developed through being socially, psychologically and linguistically proficient in their everyday lives. For them, writing this letter for a relatively unknown audience was not an exercise, but the adoption into print of life strategies. Writing was not different to living but was a means of extending living. They already possessed a set of linguistic forms which could be employed in writing. As Newkirk (1985, p. 600) said:

Because even young writers are members of interpretive communities, they can rely on shared conventions to do some of the work. I contend, then, that it is misleading to claim that children are limited to immediate audiences or to subjects close to their immediate experience. Rather, there seems to be a range of appropriations, a set of forms that young writers can use – some to address a known audience, some a more distant audience. Some are used to narrate what is happening, some to frame arguments or convey information.

Children may feel more comfortable with familiar audiences and immediate experiences, but they are not limited to them. It is undoubtedly the case that letter writing makes response to an audience easier for young children than some other genres. It enables them to draw on known life strategies more easily than, for instance, writing a scientific report. In a sustained letter writing exchange, an unknown audience soon becomes a known audience.

If the exchange for the children had been set up as an exercise where accuracy and correctness of form were paramount, then we suspect that the outcome would have been rather different. The audience would not have been Les and Nigel but the teacher: children are so proficient in understanding the true agendas of classroom life. The authenticity of the exchange made it quite distinct from most other classroom experiences. We would agree with Braig (1986, p. 112) . . .

. . . that growth in written communication competence may be, at least in part, a function of the type of written experiences and the number of encounters with functional written experiences shared by young authors.

We also agree with Stoneham (1986, p. 286) who, after setting up an authentic exchange between young American children and eighth graders, commented:

A real audience makes an enormous difference to a writer, not just as a listener but as a provider of ideas, as an encourager, as a force that makes revision more probable.

We are not trying to claim that our children knew all about, or could manifest all their understanding of, 'audience'. Could anyone? The children were inexperienced writers and had to learn and perfect many aspects of the writing craft.

In chapter 4 we were able to show that the children developed their craft in different ways, and that many of these ways had implications for their written relationship to their audience. One of the most powerful influences on the children's ability to respond to audience was that their audience answered back. It was the answering back which marked the activity as being distinct. It showed powerfully that written language can be an effective instrument for getting things done – in this instance, eliciting a reply. We are sure that part of the motivation for continuing with the exchange was that it allowed exploration in the use of a new tool.

There were three ways in which receiving replies facilitated the children's writing development. The first was that the responses from Nigel and Les were themselves demonstrations of how writers can relate to an audience. The second was that the children could experience in a very explicit way the impact of their own strategies towards their audience. The third was that they had to learn to adapt to a changing audience, for people inevitably change as time goes by.

As the letters passed to and fro, so the human relationship was constantly being redefined, and the way the writers had to respond to each other had to shift continually. This dialogic negotiation is, inevitably, under-represented in this book. We regret very much that there is insufficient space to explore more fully, through examples, the relationship between the children's and Les and Nigel's texts.

We believe that the letters written by the children show that they were able to cope with, and adapt towards, their audience very well. As their skills as authors grew, they were better able to organise their responses. But right from the start, the children were able to function dialogically. Could they do this without some sense of audience? What kind of conversation would it be if two people simply talked at each other with no regard for each other? Would it even be called dialogue? The children's letters show that they never acted in that way, even though sometimes long periods of time passed between letters and topics had been forgotten. The children were not writing essays for Les and Nigel. They were corresponding with them. They could not have done that unless there had been some underlying ability to relate to their audience.

Letter writing makes relating to audiences easier; indeed, it makes many aspects of writing easier. Part of the powerful potential of letter writing is that it mediates between a child's existing language knowledge and the ways of using written language that are characteristic of more formal written texts. It has long been an adage of educational practice that one moves from the known to the unknown. What is known at age five is how to use language orally. In particular, "Children's casual speech contains practically all the language functions necessary for getting things done in the real world" (Shuy 1988, p. 79). Children at age five are also tuned in to many aspects of social relationships. "Four year olds were even shown to have a social sensitivity which enabled them to vary their strategies for giving directives, depending on how they perceived the status of the persons to whom they addressed these directives" (op cit, p. 79).

Many forms of written language required at school make a narrow range of linguistic demands upon children, while at the same time those demands are often highly specialised. The degree of specialisation means that children are often grappling with the unknown rather than drawing upon the known. The genres of school often deny to children the right to use the language they do know. As a result, they often have to write very tentatively, or more likely, very safely. This does not mean that the letters written by the children in the sample are simply talk written down. They certainly share many relationships with talk but they move well beyond it. They link talk with literate language and allow a more gradual move towards control over the formal requirements of literate language.

Letter and dialogue journal writing allow children to employ many of their known language strategies. They can draw upon what they know about the exchanges of oral conversation, which allow them to interrogate, demand, explain, clarify, deny, apologise, joke, complain, request, categorise, argue, recount, describe, sequence, persuade, offer and ask. When these functions have to be used in letters or journals to a relatively unknown audience, children are forced to modify the oral nature of the functions. A small number of studies exist (Greene 1985, and Karelitz 1988) in which children were writing to children within the same class or school. While these were clearly very successful in many different ways, the letters and notes that resulted were very different from those written by the children in our study. They were on the whole considerably shorter and more elliptic, more linked to personal relationships and less explanatory. (For suggestions about how to use 'buddy journals' see Bromley, 1989.)

We do not accept that this is a cultural difference. We believe that it reflects a difference in the writing maturity of the respondent and relative unknownness of the audience. If children write to peers within the classroom, the notes and letters are rooted in total shared experience and the context within which they are created is part of that shared experience. What do you need to write to someone who sits on the same table, plays with you at break time, and walks home with you after school? Young children should, of course, have opportunities to write to children in their class. We are simply saying that the implications for developing as an author are considerably different if the respondent is a more mature writer.

As mature writers, Les and Nigel were able to provide more extensive demonstrations simply by being correspondents rather than as a result of deliberate instructional policy. We also think that the letters that Les and Nigel wrote scaffolded certain aspects of the children's development. As mature writers, Nigel and Les were able to make requests which elicited different and more extensive replies than might otherwise have been the case, and they could comment in ways which expanded and sustained ideas and themes initiated by the children. They were able to show how texts could be interrogated in a situation which was without threat or fear of failure for the children.

Because Les and Nigel were more distant correspondents the children had to face the fact that they could not write the same kinds of things that they would have written to a classmate. The situation drew them into attempting to be more explicit about events recorded in their letters, to offer explanations about their own activities, and to write about things in which their correspondent would be interested. The children were able to use existing conversational strategies, but at the same time were led to explore ways of organising their letters which took them beyond oral conversation.

The children behaved as letter writers from the start. That is not to say that the writing of the letters was always easy or totally success-ful, but it does mean that they took on the role with no doubts about their ability to make it work. In this respect, their efforts support the claims of Collerson (1983) and Newkirk (1985 and 1989) that children are able to cope with the technical features of the genre. In most respects, the children we worked with faced a bigger hurdle than the children examined by Collerson and Newkirk: extensive, regular and sustained written dialogue did not feature in their analyses. They were mostly concerned with a diversity of letters written for different purposes. Such letters were usually more of the one-off variety rather than dialogic. Braig (1986) did examine dialogue journal entries of seven- to nine-years-olds but, by almost totally excluding any account of her own responses, could not focus on the dialogic nature of the journals.

Young children clearly do not have to have a diet of writing experiences that are confined to stories and news recounts. A growing body of evidence reveals their ability to make forays into many different genres (Hall 1989 and Newkirk 1989). The children in our study showed vividly an astonishing confidence and competence in tackling issues of great complexity in their letter writing. The conditions that were created for them within this exchange allowed them to demonstrate success. These conditions included:

- being able to engage in authentic correspondence

- being able to pursue it over an extended period of time

- being able to choose to participate

- being given space, time and resources within the classroom

- being able to write to a distanced and relatively unknown correspondent

- being in a classroom with teachers who supported but did not interfere or try to own the correspondence

- being able to write to mature writers who were sensitive to the children's texts.

We cannot claim that such conditions will result in all children writing as the children here wrote. We do believe, however, that these conditions provide the most powerful incentives for authorship. Frank Smith talks about young people being motivated to read because they want to join the club. When children correspond under the conditions outlined above, they are becoming fully paid up members.

It is clear to us that these conditions and such correspondence have enormous benefits for children developing as authors. Now that primary school children in England and Wales have to follow a nationally determined curriculum of nine subjects, will there be room for such activities to be a central part of young children's school experience?

English of course is one of the National Curriculum subjects. The government has laid down in law the attainment targets to be studied, what counts as achieving these targets at 10 levels, and the general programmes of study that must be followed by teachers in order to achieve them. In addition, all children will be tested at ages seven and eleven using Standardised Attainment Tasks.

The government set up a committee to produce the documentation. Their two reports, *English for ages 5–11* (DES 1988) and *English for ages 5–16* (DES 1989), became the basis for *English in the national curriculum* (HMSO 1989), which represents the statutory orders that all teachers in state schools must by law follow.

In 1987 when the children started writing letters, there were no national programmes of study, no national attainment targets and no standardised assessment tasks. Yet the ways in which the children worked with Anne, and the conditions outlined above, anticipated to quite a degree what has subsequently appeared in the National Curriculum English. This is not coincidence. All three of us held views which reflected contemporary thinking about literacy education, and these same beliefs underpin many aspects of *English in the National Curriculum*. In addition, all three of us had been involved in the Manchester section of the National Writing Project where we specifically considered young children's writing. The government committee which produced the documentation were certainly influenced by the evidence of the National Writing Project. But to what extent does the National Curriculum allow teachers to involve the children in dialogic letter writing?

At Key Stage One (5–7 years) pupils should 'undertake a range of chronological writing including some at least of diaries, stories, letters . . .' (Programmes of Study 17). It is not until Key Stage 2 (7–11 years) that they should: 'have opportunities to write personal letters to real known participants and should be shown how to set them out' (DES, 1989 17.41(iv)).

Presumably the letter writing that should occur at Key Stage One is not seen as real letter writing. This view is shared by many parents. A survey of over 400 parents of young children (Hall et al 1989) revealed that most parents felt that children had to reach seven, eight or nine, to write a letter unassisted.

In general terms, *English in the National Curriculum* supports many of the features of our exchange. There are many references to the importance of having experience of a wide range of genres and a variety of audiences. Most important, the emphasis in the document is on the authoring rather than the secretarial experience of writing. Attainment target 3, the major attainment target to do with writing, is 'a growing ability to construct and convey meaning in written language matching style to audience and purpose'. This could be said to be exactly what this book is about.

English for ages 5–11 points out that there is no simple transition from spoken to written language. As indicated earlier in this chapter, letter writing provides a perfect bridge between spoken and written language. Unfortunately, none of the documentation refers to what is for us a very significant and beneficial factor in becoming a writer: the interactive experience of letters and dialogue journals.

Nevertheless, we believe that letter writing as an authentic and sustained activity is both supported and encouraged by the National Curriculum. The programmes of study for writing begin with the sentence: 'Pupils should have frequent opportunities to write in different contexts and for a variety of purposes and audiences, including themselves.' (Programmes of study 13.)

Letter writing is one way of achieving that objective. It is not the only way but it deserves to feature in the repertoire of 'purpose and audiences' recommended by the National Curriculum.

The possibilities for generating authentic letter writing experiences are very wide (Hall and Robinson, in press). Children can write to older children within their school or to children in other schools, including schools abroad. They can write to a variety of adult audiences, in particular elderly people who may have more time on their hands and be delighted to correspond with young people. Letters do not have to be simply sent by post. There are many computer networks that allow transmission of messages, and it will not be long before fax machines have their place in schools alongside computers and typewriters. The advantages of fax are that children can easily send handwritten letters, can include drawings and diagrams, and can retain the originals.

The children with whom we have worked have educated us. Through their efforts, we have been able to understand more fully how children develop as authors. More important, we have been able to strengthen our beliefs that young children have considerable competencies with written language when the situations in which they work allow them the opportunities to display their authorship.

We think all the children are wonderful. They readily agreed to write to us, they regularly keep us interested and amused, they put up with our meanderings, our interruptions and our occasional visits to talk to them. Watching them grow as people and authors has been a quite extraordinary experience. We hope the experience has not finished yet. We feel privileged to know these children, and we hope that one day they will see this book as a tribute to them. One of the children wrote in a letter:

And I'll always be your friend.

Friendship is the finest possible reason for writing to someone, and it is what we feel towards all the children.

APPENDIX

LETTERS FROM NIGEL AND LES

In order to give readers some idea of the way in which Nigel and Les replied to the children, we reproduce two letters by each of them.

This letter from Nigel was in response to Mark's letter, reproduced on page 43.

Thankyou for another lovely long letter. I am very well but two of my snakes have been ill. I had to take them to the vet. He gave me some medicine for them. It was very difficult to make them take. They are better now.

I am sending a copy of one of my stories to Mrs Robinson. She will show it to you.

Please do write and tell me what you think of. Is it a good story?

In your letter you said that Friday is your favourite day. I expect it is Mrs Robinson's favourite day. Can you think why?

Do write to me again

Best wishes

Nigel

This was in response to Elizabeth's letter, reproduced on page 83.

Thankyou for two very lovely letters. You write very interesting letters and I always enjoy reading them.

I was very pleased that you had a wonderful birthday. You are very lucky to have a TV in your room. Does that mean you can watch TV while you are in bed.

I watched lots of TV during Easter. I also have a TV in the bedroom but I do not often watch that. It is a black and white TV and I prefer to stay downstairs and watch it in colour.

I am going to fly to Brussels in a week's time. Brussels is in Belgium. I am going to give a talk to some teachers. I am looking forward to going as I haven't been to Brussels for fifteen years. I wonder if it will have changed in that time.

I will tell you all about it in my next letter.

Best wishes

Nigel

This letter from Les responds to the children's concern about his sporting activities on the ice (see page 94).

I'm so glad Father Christmas left you lots of presents. You were lucky, allright!

I think you can have a good holiday just staying at home, don't you? I'm going to have a wee holiday soon and just stay at home and sleepin every day and do what I want!

Don't worry about the ice 'I DON'T go on it unless it is at least 12 inches deep! Then even cars can drive on it! Did you know that in Minnesota - people even have ice houses on the lakes. You can sit in them and have a fire and keep warm and fish down a hole drilled in the deep ice! When it is this cold outside -20°, the ice doesn't crack!

Be sure to write again soon and let me know what you've been doing.   Love,
                                        Les

P.s Thanks for your hugs and kisses!

Les sent this letter to the child who had been to the United States when she was a baby (see page 94).

I'm so happy to hear you had such a good time in Wales! It was nice that you were able to meet other girls. Other children can easily see what a lovely person you are and want to make friends with you.

My, I loved your poem. I could really see people walking in the woods on the leaves and hear the sounds they made as they stepped on the leaves.

What kind of a t-shirt do you have from Minneapolis? What does it say? I'm sending some cards from Des Moines, Iowa, where Nigel and I were in October. Did you go there, too?

An America holiday is coming November 26th. We call it Thanksgiving. It comes from the feast the Pilgrims had to give thanks for living through a terrible winter and having a good harvest (like Harvest Home) They invited the Indians to come who had helped them learn how to live in this country. 92 come. I hope my daughter will come home for it. We usually have a Turkey dinner. Write soon,

Love, Les

BIBLIOGRAPHY

BRAIG, D 'Six characters in search of an audience' in Schieffelin, B and Gilmore, P (eds), *The acquisition of literacy: ethnographic perspectives,* pp. 110–31 (Norwood, NJ: Ablex Publishing Corporation, 1986)

BROMLEY, K 'Buddy journals make the reading-writing connection', *The Reading Teacher,* vol 43(2), pp. 122–29, 1989

COLLERSON, J 'One child and one genre: developments in letter writing' in Kroll, B and Wells, G (eds), *Explorations in the development of writing,* pp. 71–93 (Chichester: Wiley, 1983)

COLLINS, J and MICHAELS, S 'Speaking and writing: discourse stragegies and the acquisition of literacy' in Cook-Gumperz, J (ed), *The social construction of literacy,* pp. 207–221 (Cambridge: Cambridge University Press, 1986)

Department of Education and Science, *English for ages 5–11* (London: DES, 1988)

– *English for ages 5–16* (London, DES, 1989)

DONALDSON, M *Children's minds* (London: Fontana, 1978)

DUFFY, R 'Dear Mrs Duffy' in Hall, N (ed), *Writing with reason: the emergence of authorship in young children,* pp. 38–55 (Sevenoaks: Hodder and Stoughton, 1989)

GRAVES, D *Writing: teachers and children at work* (Portsmouth, NH: Heinemann Educational Books, 1983)

GREENE, J 'Children's writing in an elementary school postal system' in Farr, M (ed), *Advances in writing research Vol 1. Children's early writing development* (Norwood, N J: Ablex Publishing Corporation, 1985)

HALL, N *Writing with reason: the emergence of authorship in young children* (Sevenoaks: Hodder and Stoughton, 1989; published in the USA by Heinemann Educational Books, Inc, 1989)

HALL, N and DUFFY, R 'Every child has a story to tell', *Language Arts,* vol 64(5) 1987, pp. 523–29

HALL, N, HERRING, G, HENN, H and CRAWFORD, L *Parental views on writing and the teaching of writing* (Manchester: Department of Educational Studies, Manchester Polytechnic, 1989)

HALL, N and ROBINSON, A *Keeping in touch: interactive writing with young children* (London: Mary Glasgow Publications, in press)

HARSTE, J, WOODWARD, V and BURKE, C 'Examining our instructional assumptions', *Research in the teaching of English*, vol 18(1) pp. 84–108.

HMSO, *English in the National Curriculum*, (London: HMSO 1989)

KARELITZ, E 'Note writing: a neglected genre' in Newkirk, T and Atwell, N (eds), *Understanding writing: ways of observing, learning and teaching* (Portsmouth, NH: Heinemann Educational Books, 1988)

KROLL, B 'Audience adaptation in children's persuasive letters', *Written Communication*, vol 1(4) 1984, pp. 407–27.

NEWKIRK, T 'The hedgehog or the fox: the dilemma of writing development', *Language Arts*, vol 62(6) 1985, pp. 593–603

NEWKIRK, T – *More than stories: the range of children's writing* (Portsmouth, NH: Heinemann Educational Books, 1989)

NIGROSH, G *Audience in children's letter writing: a study of sociolinguistic development*, Unpublished PhD thesis (Providence, RI: Brown University, 1985)

ROBINSON, A 'But we still believe in Father Christmas' in Hall, N (ed), *Writing with reason: the emergence of authorship in young children*, pp. 87–99 (Sevenoaks: Hodder and Stoughton, 1989)

ROSEN, H 'Towards a language policy across the curriculum' in Barnes, D, Britton, J and Rosen, H (eds), *Language, the learner and the school* (London: Penguin Books, 1971)

ROWCROFT, V 'Young letter writers as authors' in Hall, N (ed), *Writing with reason: the emergence of authorship in young children* pp. 21–37 (Sevenoaks: Hodder and Stoughton, 1989)

SHUY, R 'The oral basis for dialogue journals' in Staton, J, Shuy, R, Kreeft Peyton, J and Reed, L (eds), *Dialogue journal communication: classroom, linguistic, social and cognitive views* (Norwood, NJ: Ablex, Publishing Corporation, 1988)

STONEHAM, J 'What happens when students have a real audience?' *Journal of teaching writing*, vol 5(2) 1986, pp. 281–87

VARGUS, N *Socio-cognitive constraints in transaction: letter writing over time*, Unpublished PhD thesis (Indiana University: 1983)

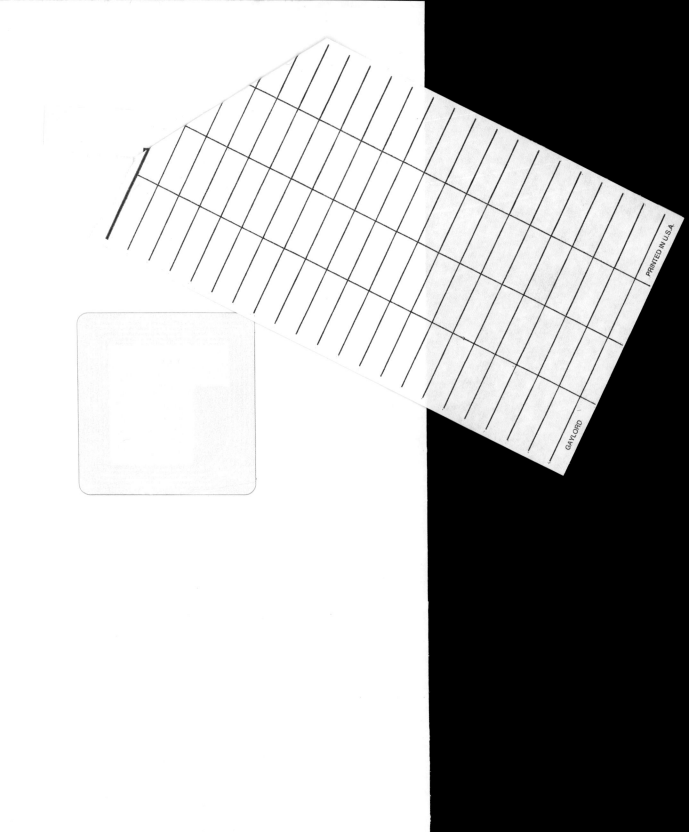